CW00458673

THE WORLD'S MOST
**SENSATIONAL
ASSASSINATIONS**

THE WORLD'S MOST
SENSATIONAL
ASSASSINATIONS

BY
NIGEL BLUNDELL

SUNBURST BOOKS

PHOTOGRAPHY CREDITS

Contents

Introduction

The word assassin conjures up a sinister picture of a cold-blooded, calculating killer. What differentiates an assassin from other murderers is the determination to wipe from the face of the earth a fellow human being whose ideas and ideals conflict with his or her own.

Be it revenge plotted by one single, obsessive mind, or deadly revolt perpetrated by fanatics, the sole aim is to exterminate at any cost.

But where and when did assassinations begin? The word 'assassin' derives from the Arabic 'hashashin' literally meaning 'hashish eaters'. It was used to describe a sect of Shi'ite Muslims feared throughout 11th century Persia for their bloody elimination of all political opponents.

The centuries have seen many great politicians and leaders struck down, many fine men and women eliminated. Here, in *The World's Most Sensational Assassinations*, are accounts of just a few of the greatest people who perished in the name of politics and power.

All had different dreams. All had visions for the future. Assassination robbed them of their chance to change the world - but guaranteed that their names live on for ever.

Julius Caesar

The assassination of Caius Julius Caesar on 15th March, 44 BC did not just assure him of the title of the most famous Roman who ever lived. It also, ironically, secured the future of the Roman Empire - opposition to which was the motive for his murder.

It was the ultimate political bungle, for in killing Caesar, the conspirators ensured that the old Republic, which they sought to uphold, would be replaced by a new kind of monarchy, the very thing that they hoped to avoid.

Their view was that Caesar had to die, because he was already a king in all but name, and that hated title was virtually within his grasp. Ever since the last king of Rome, Tarquin the Proud, had been deposed in 509 BC, Rome had been a Republic governed by the Senate and two consuls appointed for a period of one year. For centuries this system had worked well, although in the event of a national emergency it was possible to nominate a 'dictator' who could be given special powers for up to six months.

At the end of the second century BC, however, these powers were exploited by a succession of men. One leading general, Caius Marius (incidentally a relative of Caesar) was elected consul seven times despite the law requiring a ten year gap between consulships. In 86 BC, the last year of his life, he perpetrated dreadful acts of reprisal against his enemies.

In 82 BC, his rival, Sulla, seized power after marching on Rome with an army and likewise wreaked bloody vengeance on his enemies during his three year term as consul. As a result of this period of unrest the Senate banned all Roman generals from bringing their armies into Italy and they were forbidden to cross the River Rubicon.

The assassination of Julius Caesar - 'the noblest
Roman of them all'.

However, it became clear that political power in Rome could be obtained by those with a disregard for the old system, a ruthless ambition and, most important, an army. Julius Caesar was such a man.

Caesar was elected dictator for the first time in 49 BC after refusing to disband the army with which he had conquered Gaul (France). When he eventually became the first general to defy the laws of the Senate and crossed the Rubicon, the Senate and the Republicans appointed Pompey, Caesar's old ally and one-time son-in-law to lead an armed opposition to Caesar.

However, when Pompey was defeated by Caesar and subsequently murdered after fleeing to Egypt, Caesar's position looked secure, the more so after he had pardoned his former enemies and been appointed dictator for the second time in 47 BC. In 45 BC he was made dictator 'perpetuus' (dictator for life). He was king in all but name.

Although Caesar was worshipped by the common people, constitutionalists foresaw in Caesar the return of the hated monarchy. By 44 BC they had decided that, if the old constitution were to survive, then Caesar would have to be removed.

In 53 BC, a Roman army commanded by Crassus had been completely destroyed by the Paprthians at Carrhae. The disaster was still unavenged in 44 BC when Caesar began to make preparations for a campaign. The date of embarkation was set for 18th March.

On the 15th, the Ides of March, Caesar made his way to the Senate to obtain the Senate's blessing for the campaign. He disregarded the warning which he had received from a soothsayer a few weeks before to: 'Beware the Ides of March.' He also ignored his wife Calpurnia's plea that he should stay at home, after she had had a dreadful nightmare in which she had seen her husband brutally murdered.

Caesar did not fear death. He had consistently refused to employ a bodyguard saying 'There is nothing more unfortunate than a permanent guard, which is a sign of ever-present death.' On another occasion, he had stated 'It is better to die once than to be always expecting death.'

On the evening of 14th March, he dined with his horse master, Lepidus, and commented that the most pleasant death was a sudden and unexpected one. Caesar was not to be disappointed.

There were at least sixty conspirators in the plot to murder Caesar. Principal among them were Caius Cassius, Caius Trebonius, Decimus Brutus and Caesar's great friend, Marcus Brutus, who, according to legend, was a descendant of Lucius Junius Brutus who had deposed the last king. While Caius Trebonius detained Caesar's lieutenant and close confidant Mark Antony in an ante-room in the hall of Pompey's theatre where the Senate had assembled, Caesar was surrounded by his enemies and stabbed twenty-three times. Wrapped in his blood-soaked toga, he collapsed silently, ironically beneath a statue of Pompey.

It was later discovered that only one of the wounds could have been fatal. It is not known whether that wound was inflicted by Brutus or whether Caesar's alleged dying words 'Et tu, Brute' owe more to Shakespeare's poetic imagination than to historical fact.

What is certain is that, far from achieving their goal of restoring the old order, the conspirators only succeeded in bringing another thirteen years of civil war to the Roman world, to be followed by the establishment of a Roman royal family - the very thing they had sought to avoid.

In the immediate aftermath of the assassination, they

were dismayed to find that, instead of receiving the gratitude of the population, they were met everywhere with shock and condemnation. Caesar's will made his nephew, Octavian, his heir, and it was he who, with his ally Mark Antony, emerged victorious from the civil war. There was no opposition when Octavian appointed himself 'Princeps' (First Citizen). Rome was simply glad that the war was over.

In addition, in 27 BC he adopted the title Augustus Caesar; the period of the Roman Empire had begun. The term Caesar came to mean emperor, and has endured in the modern derivation, Czar or Tsar.

Julius Caesar - soldier, statesman, historian, orator, poet, philosopher and mathematician - was a great man during his life. In death, to quote Shakespeare, he was 'the noblest Roman of them all'.

Caligula

When Caligula took up the reins of power in Rome, the people rejoiced, for he had stepped into the sandals of Tiberius, a debauched sadist and master of vicious palace politics who killed for kicks.

Caligula's ascent to emperor was seen as an end to the bad old days of orgies and bloodlust. Within a few months, this optimism and the hopes and dreams of those Romans who yearned for a better way lay in tatters. Caligula had learned all he knew at the knee of the master who had tormented them for so long. He matured into an ogre as bad, if not worse, than his predecessor.

Tiberius was a former army general who had earned the respect and support of Emperor Augustus by quelling rebellions around the extensive Roman Empire. At first, he displayed a measured attitude which boded well for the Romans, sidestepping any conflicts which were not essential and which would have cost thousands of lives.

His great talent lay in handling money. Thanks to tax reforms and some ambitious book-keeping, Tiberius swelled the imperial coffers to unprecendented amounts. He was, however, sickened by the back-biting to which he was subjected constantly. To escape, he left Rome in favour of picturesque Capri, from where he ruled at arm's length, relying on his right-hand man, Sejanus, to do his bidding in the capital.

As Tiberius loosened the noose of power that he found so stifling, he also relaxed the moral manacles. The next few years saw the Empire's rapid decline into licentiousness and dubious sexual practices.

Tiberius then suffered a great personal tragedy when his son, Drusus, was poisoned. It was several years before

The tyrant Caligula.

Tiberius realised that his trusted adviser, Sejanus, was behind the death of Drusus. His revenge was swift.

Outraged, the Emperor demanded that the Roman Senate execute Sejanus, by now the most powerful figure in Rome. The sentence was carried out immediately. Sejanus was strangled and his corpse was held up for ridicule in Rome for three days afterwards. The family of Sejanus was also killed, including his 14-year-old daughter. The treachery appeared to unleash a killing fervour in Tiberius, who now condemned to death anyone under the slightest suspicion for even the most trivial of offences. As these mass slaughters continued, his popularity slumped.

In his declining years Tiberius named the young Caligula as his successor. Caligula, awkward and ugly, served an informal apprenticeship under the ageing Emperor on Capri, although why Tiberius chose him as his successor still is not clear. Tiberius himself remarked 'I am nursing a viper in Rome's bosom.'

When Tiberius fell ill, Caligula dashed to his side and removed the imperial signet ring from his finger with undue haste. To his successor's horror, Tiberius revived. Helped by Macro, successor to Sejanus, Caligula smothered the ailing emperor with a pillow. Now the glittering reward was within his grasp.

Caligula did much to make himself popular with the people as his rule got underway. He pledged to end the phoney treason trials which had claimed so many lives under Tiberius. He reinstated the gladiatorial games outlawed by his predecessor and launched a series of extravagant festivals.

Yet the masses who were hoping for a brighter and braver new world knew nothing of his personal torment. Caligula, born on 31st August, 12 AD, was the son of

Germanicus Caesar and Agrippina the Elder. He and his five brothers and sisters knew little of cosy family life. Most members of his immediate family had been murdered or banished from the Empire after incurring the wrath of Tiberius. In fact, special laws were passed to penalise the descendants of his father. These grim occurrences during his early life had soured the soul of the new Emperor who chose to hide behind a facade of generosity until he found the opportunity to wreak a terrible revenge.

Among the first to feel the chill of his anger was the loyal Macro. Although Caligula had been aided immeasurably by him during his ascent to power, he was now dismissed as '.... the teacher of one who no longer needs to learn.' Caligula, who had enjoyed a long affair with Macro's wife, had him killed for pimping.

Caligula's race to claim the imperial signet ring had been due in no small part to the fact that another man had been named joint heir. It wasn't long before the unfortunate Tiberius Gemellus, who lost that vital initiative, was put to death along with his entire family.

The new Emperor made a sport out of condemning his closest advisers and admirers. He described Rome as '.... a city of necks waiting for me to chop them.' In a bloody witchhunt he probed the old papers of the cases which had been brought against members of his family years earlier and had those involved killed without mercy.

Executioners were asked to make all killings a spectacle, as long and drawn out as possible. Caligula favoured a theatrical flourish to the death throes, having arms and legs chopped off or tongues hacked out before the blessed release of death. No-one was safe from his macabre desires. 'Off comes this beautiful head whenever I give the word,' he would coo.

He married four times, once forbidding an ex-wife ever to have sex again. Yet his own sexual adventures were infamous. He would bed anyone he desired, sending divorce papers to the husbands of his married female quarry. Favourite among his lovers, however, were his three surviving sisters, particularly Drusilla whom he compelled to divorce her husband and marry him. When she died, he mourned for months and made it a capital offence to laugh.

His promiscuity was not confined to women. Men were also among the many to visit his chambers, knowing that to spurn the Emperor's advances meant certain death.

But perhaps his greatest crime against the empire was his abuse of the treasury. The prudent Tiberius had left it overflowing with cash, an estimated 2.7 billion sesterces. Caligula spent the lot and more besides. His frills and thrills left the empire broke. He insisted on bathing in perfume instead of water. He hosted feasts which cost 10 million sesterces apiece and threw cash at the lucky few to find favour with him.

He never forgot how a fortune teller had once told him that he had as much chance of becoming Emperor as he did of riding a horse over the waters of the Bay of Baiae. Now he decided to do just that. He had two lines of ships anchored along the waterway and covered with planks to provide a bridlepath. So many ships were needed to fulfil the command that many trading vessels were pulled out of service and others had to be built. Caligula had his wish and trotted up and down the three-mile stretch several times before he grew bored. The effect of this whim on the balance of trade in the empire was catastrophic.

Short of funds, he taxed food and wages. Even the earnings of prostitutes were not exempt. A short cut to extra cash which he used often was to accuse a rich man of treason. The fellow was killed and his wealth went to the state.

Finally, Caligula awarded himself the status of god. First, he impersonated a variety of Roman male gods. Later, he took to dressing in women's clothes, claiming to be Diana or Venus. With every member of his court suspected of treason, Caligula went on to honour his loyal horse, Incitatus. The animal was kept in a lavish marble stall complete with an ivory manger for straw. The demented Emperor announced that he was preparing to make Incitatus his chosen successor.

There appeared to be no question that Caligula was quite mad. In those traitorous times, it was not too long before someone plotted to destroy him. In utmost secrecy a group of Senators and high-ranking members of the national guard decided to assassinate Caligula, parasite of the empire.

His four year rule came to an end on 24th January, 41 AD on the final day of the Palatine Games. It was the morning after Caligula had announced that he had had a dream in which Zeus, king of the gods, had kicked him out of heaven.

In a secret passage leading from his palace to the arena, the band of killers, led by one embittered Tribune member, Cassius Chaerea, stabbed Caligula to death. He suffered more than thirty wounds, dying in the half-light of the narrow walkway.

As news of his death circulated, many feared a trick. If they celebrated the death of the deadly tyrant, would he appear and charge them with treason? Bold guards confirmed the glad news when they killed his wife and daughter. Rome was liberated from a tyrant once more.

English Kings

U neasy lies the head that wears a crown,' said the king in Shakespeare's *Henry IV*. And none could have known better than he. He had just murdered Richard II, the rightful king, and stolen his throne. But intrigue and assassination have walked hand in hand through every court in Britain since the Norman Conquest of 1066. And the first victim was the second king, William Rufus.

William the Conqueror left his dukedom of Normandy to his eldest son, Robert, and his kingdom of England to his third son, William. His fourth son, Henry, merely received a small sum of money and his second son, Richard, was already dead. Already the seeds of strife and fratricide had been sown.

William II, named Rufus for his red-faced, debauched countenance, was unquestionably a politician, and as unscrupulous and unprincipled as any of that breed. Much of his oppressive reign was spent plotting and fighting against his brothers, as well as numerous other foes. He was a ruthless and malignant man, much given to cruelty and the selfish indulgence of personal pleasures.

The critical moment for William Rufus came in 1096 when his brother, Robert, decided to go on a crusade to the Holy Land. To finance the war, he mortgaged his dukedom to William. The brothers swore that if either died childless, the other would inherit all his lands and titles. This deal was still uppermost in the mind of their brother, Henry, four years later, when a royal party was out hunting in the New Forest.

Suddenly an arrow hummed through the air and

embedded itself in William's black heart. Ostensibly it was an accident, and it was widely regarded as such, although many in the kingdom felt it might have been a merciful intervention by God. The man who fired the fatal bolt was Walter Tirrel, a member of the party.

But the evidence points to the real guilt of William's younger, dispossessed brother Henry, who immediately galloped to London to seize the treasury and have himself crowned king, leaving William's body to lie where it fell. He acted because it was his last chance to seize the kingdom. William's appointed heir, his other brother Robert, was due back from the Crusades within a month - and, as he was bringing a wife, there was a real danger of another legitimate heir to add to the chain which would distance Henry even further from the coveted throne of England.

Edward II was the most famous royal assassination victim, mainly because of the unforgettable death scene in Christopher Marlowe's play, where the dispossessed king is murdered by having a red-hot poker thrust deep into his posterior - which was considered at the time to be a fitting death for a heretic and a sodomite. Whether or not he was completely homosexual is a moot point. He fathered four children by his French wife, Isabella, and at least one by another woman. But he was never considered to be a true man like his father. Edward I had hammered the Welsh and Scots into submission and was indomitable both in war and politics. His son, although of strong, muscular build, was weak, indecisive and incompetent.

During his reign, the Scots, led by Robert the Bruce, threw off the English yoke and even made inroads into England. However it was Edward II's dalliance with his court favourite, the Gascon, Piers Gaveston, that caused most of the hostility towards him both at court and amongst the people of the country.

At the start of his reign in 1307, Gaveston was already in exile, having been thrown out of England by Edward I. Young Edward II's first act as king was to recall him. It is highly likely that Edward and Gaveston were lovers - certainly Queen Isabella, the fiery Frenchwoman whom Edward had married when she was just 12, thought so. She didn't stop plotting against Gaveston until he was dead. And since Edward then transferred his affections to Hugh Despenser, son of the ambitious Earl of Winchester, she continued her scheming - only now she despaired of her husband, and plotted to oust him.

Whilst England faced humiliation at Bannockburn and even a brief civil war, during which law and order largely broke down all across the land, Edward continued lavishing gifts and estates on the Despensers to the fury of the English nobles. But while everyone hoped that someone would put an end to the reign of the woeful monarch, no-one expected that it would be the king's wife who would finally bring about his death.

Arrested as an alien on the outbreak of war with France in 1324, she was finally sent to France to help negotiate a truce between her husband and her brother, Charles IV. It was a fatal error. On the continent, she mingled with all the English exiles and malcontents, taking as her lover and fellow plotter Roger Mortimer, who had escaped from the Tower of London on the morning scheduled for his own execution.

The pair returned to England in 1326 with a handful of followers as support for the king melted away. Edward panicked and fled with the Despensers to Wales. The elder

Despenser surrendered at Bristol and was rapidly executed. Edward and his favourite, the younger Despenser, tried to make their escape by sailing out to sea, but were blown back to land, where they were captured by Henry of Lancaster, whose brother Thomas had been executed by Edward. Despenser was tortured and died a slow death. Edward was sent in chains to Kenilworth, where he remained in a foul dungeon while his wife set about deposing him.

By 1327 the Bishops, Abbots and Barons who made up the parliament had voted to depose the king in favour of his heir, Edward. But since Edward III was still a child, the real power would be Isabella's and Mortimer's. Edward II met his end at Berkeley Castle, where he was confined in a chamber even more foul than that at Kenilworth.

How he really died will never be known, although he was certainly murdered by agents of his wife. The story of the red-hot poker was first recounted some thirty years later by the chronicler, Geoffrey le Baker, and it would not be unlikely that the king was tortured before his death. So once again the people rejoiced, as they had at the death of William Rufus.

Edward's great grandson was the next to die at the hand of an assassin. Richard II died ignominiously - some say bravely - in 1400.

Son of the Black Prince and the Fair Maid of Kent, he came to the throne on the death of Edward III, as his father had already died in battle. Like Edward II, Richard's sexuality was never entirely clear. A vain and effeminate man, he loved bright clothes and surrounded himself with fawning courtiers. He could, nevertheless, be impressive when the need arose. When little more than a boy, he rode with a small entourage to meet thousands of angry, revolutionary serfs when the Peasants' Revolt swept through Kent and reached London. And he quelled it almost single-handedly. After the Mayor of London had struck down the obnoxious Wat Tyler, Richard rode forward and made a string of promises that persuaded the peasants to return home.

It was his finest hour. It may even be that he intended to keep his promises. That he did not was of little account to the barons. It was when he continued to vacillate and broke his promises to them that a number of them decided to act.

Henry Bolingbroke, another grandson of Edward III, by his younger son, John of Gaunt, imprisoned Richard and declared himself Henry IV. Parliament, with the exception of a few brave dissenters, ratified the succession and Richard was locked away in Pontefract, where, ironically, it was the actions of his supporters that sealed his fate.

Two failed uprisings persuaded the new king that it was too dangerous to let Richard live. Nowadays it is difficult to distinguish fact from propaganda in those turbulent early days of the Wars of the Roses. The Yorkist faction held that Richard was deliberately starved to death, the Lancastrians that he had refused food and had starved himself. But at least Richard had survived childhood - no mean feat for a king who happened to be a minor.

Edward V, who died in 1483, was not so lucky. Edward was murdered, probably suffocated, at the age of 13, along with his brother Richard, Duke of York. What became known as the murder of the Princes in the Tower presented a mystery which was only solved this century. After five hundred years, guilt has never been proven, though the evidence points to Richard III, the notorious 'Crookback Dick', the former Duke of Gloucester.

Richard had been a fiercely loyal subject of his brother Edward IV. He had fought for him against the Scots and against the Lancastrians, winning great renown. He had even been heavily involved in the killing of Henry VI, when he succeeded in deposing Edward for a short time. But Edward had married a commoner, Elizabeth Wydville, and in giving lands and titles to her relatives, he had antagonised the older nobility and set up a separate faction at court. Richard was one of those who feared and distrusted the Wydvilles. As a result, he rarely came to court, and built his power base in York.

While Richard was never as black as he was painted by Sir Thomas More and Shakespeare, both of whom had to please their Tudor masters, there is little doubt that he was a schemer and, eventually, a killer. However the death of his other brother, the Duke of Clarence, who was drowned in a butt of Malmsey wine, was not of his doing, as Shakespeare suggests. Clarence had been tried and condemned on several counts of treason against Edward IV, and drowning was the method of execution he chose for himself. Nevertheless, Richard, who was quarrelling with Clarence over land and over Ann Neville, whom he married, did not lift a finger to defend his brother.

On the death of Edward IV in 1483, Richard had been named Protector for the period of 13-year-old Edward V's minority. Whether he had intended to seize the throne all along, or whether he acted out of self-preservation in the face of the open malice of the Wydvilles cannot be known, but from the beginning, he acted as if he were king.

His first act was to get young Edward V out of his

mother's hands. Having achieved this by tricking the boy's guardian, he set about getting hold of his other nephew, the Duke of York. Here, however, he had some difficulty, as Edward IV's widow had gone into holy sanctuary in Westminster Abbey with her family. While he could not breach the sanctuary, Richard hounded the Queen Mother until she agreed to let her younger son join his brother for the Coronation.

The two Princes were housed in the Tower of London. At that time this was not the dark keep and prison-house it was to become under the Tudors. It was both England's premier fortress and a royal residence. The princes would have lived well there. However, after two months, as the date for the Coronation drew close, Richard postponed it indefinitely. He had decided that Edward V would quickly fall under his mother's influence again and would take some revenge on the uncle who had kidnapped him.

At the same time Richard removed Edward's guardians and friends and later had them executed. Edward and his brother were alone and at the mercy of this tyrant.

Richard began his campaign for the throne by declaring his brother, Edward IV, a bastard. That he was grossly slandering his mother, who still lived, deterred him not at all, though he subsequently dropped the charge because no-one believed it.

His next tactic was to declare that Edward IV's children by Elizabeth Wydville were illegitimate, because his marriage with her was bigamous. This was more plausible, as Edward IV was a noted womaniser. There are, however, no records to prove the charge, and most historians have dismissed it. If Edward V were declared a bastard, Richard's claim to the throne would have had some validity, because the son of his elder brother Clarence had already been

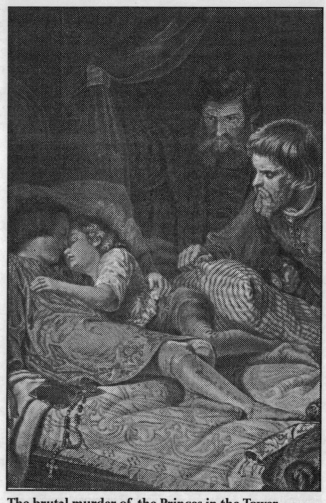

The brutal murder of the Princes in the Tower.

barred from succession because of his father's treason. In any event, another king had won power by illicit means.

The true king, however, was not without friends, and there were uprisings in his support. Richard was always ahead of the game. His spies were everywhere. On the other hand, he now realised that the Princes in the Tower had to be removed. While they lived, they were always going to be a threat. So he appointed Sir James Tyrell (the name, curiously is the same as that of the slayer of William Rufus, although no relationship can be traced) to do the deed. And Tyrell, over-ambitious for promotion, according to Sir Thomas More, brought in two accomplices to smother the young princes. They then disposed of the bodies in a hole they dug beneath a stairwell.

Tyrell was later to confess his part in the assassination to his new master, Henry VII, but the princes' bodies were not recovered, probably because Tyrell did not witness the murder and hurried away straight afterwards. He probably believed they had been taken elsewhere for burial.

It was not until 1674 - one hundred and ninety years later - that two skeletons were discovered by workmen clearing rubble for King Charles II. Experts at the time were convinced that the workmen had unearthed the bones of Edward V and his brother, Richard, and they were given a state burial in Westminster Abbey. There they remained undisturbed until 1934, when Dr. Lawrence Tanner and Professor W. Wright, a dental surgeon, examined them again and declared them to be the skeletons of two related youngsters aged 13 and 10. They also revealed that the elder had been suffering from the painful bone disease, osteomyelitis (Edward had been receiving extensive treatment for a medical condition before he disappeared from sight), and that a red stain on one of the skulls was a blood stain caused during the act of suffocation.

The age of the victims at death is important, as it dates their murder to 1483. And thus the man responsible could only have been the renegade Richard III.

Whenever a king was killed, it was in somebody's interest to say that he was really still alive. Legends persisted for a number of years that both Edward II and Richard II had escaped death.

Edward, the story goes, killed a porter as he escaped from Berkeley Castle, and this man's body was buried in place of his own. A Genoese priest, Manuel Fieschi, claimed to have heard the confession of Edward several years after he was supposed to have died. After a period in Ireland, Edward was said to have gone to France, where he was received by the Pope at Avignon. He then travelled to Italy and became a hermit. Fieschi was a Papal notary, so unlikely to lie - although he could have been duped into lying as part of a hoax for someone else's political ends.

The case for Richard escaping is even less likely, although he did have a double, Richard Maudeleyn, in his court entourage, and this man was certainly killed in the 1400 uprisings. Rumour had it that his body was substituted for Richard II's, after which the ex-king made his escape from Pontefract and found sanctuary in Scotland. When the Earl of Northumberland rebelled against Henry IV in 1403, his aim, according to his manifesto, was to restore Richard II.

It is impossible to know how good a ruler Edward V would have been. However, his death brought about the fall of the House of York, the end of the Wars of the Roses, and the start of the Tudor dynasty, without which the Church of England might never have come into being.

Henry IV of France

The assassination of Henry IV of France in 1610 saved France and, indeed, the whole of Europe from the most disastrous war it had ever faced. And all over a 15-year-old girl.

In 1589 Henry had ended a five year period of turbulence known as the War of the Three Henries, during which the childless Henry III had fought for the throne against two rivals, Henry of Guise and Henry of Navarre. Guise seemed to be on the point of winning the battle, when Henry III had him murdered. A matter of months later, the King himself was murdered, leaving Navarre to become Henry IV on the back of not one, but two assassinations.

Henry, first of the Bourbon line of kings, had been brought up in the new, Protestant faith. Following the St. Bartholomew's Day massacre of 1579, however, in which many leading Calvinists had perished, he rapidly converted to Catholicism, only to revert subsequently to Protestantism. On becoming King, he found no difficulty in embracing the Roman faith once again.

Two things he loved more than his religion were warfare and women. As a military strategist, he proved himself supreme in France. As a womaniser he was a legend. His mistresses grew younger as he matured. In 1610, the year of his death, his fancy was caught by an amorous 15-year-old called Charlotte. For her, Henry was prepared to embroil France in what promised to be a long, expensive and extremely bitter war.

In March, 1609 the duchies of Cleves, Julich and Berg were left without a duke. As rival claimants squared up to each other, Protestant forces marched in to obstruct the Holy Roman Empire. They appealed to Henry for help, but at first he vacillated. However, when the Prince de Conde suddenly married Henry's mistress, Charlotte, and eloped with her to Brussels, his mind was made up. He vowed to march into Belgium at the head of fifty thousand men, and at the same time he offered his support to the Protestants of Cleves against the Spaniards.

So Europe stood on the brink of a cataclysmic war that would have embroiled France, Spain, the Holy Roman Empire and various German and Italian states.

On 14th May, 1610, as Europe prepared for the conflict, Henry was travelling by coach to meet his chief minister at the arsenal. The whole of Paris was covered in bunting and decorations ready for the entry of his newly crowned Queen, Marie de Medici. As the carriage slowed in the traffic, a large, red-headed man called Ravaillac leapt onto the running board.

The assassin produced a dagger, leaned into the carriage and was able to stab at the King three times before being overpowered. It was enough. One of the blows had pierced Henry's lung, and he died within minutes of being rushed to the Louvre.

His death caused instability in France, because his son, Louis XIII, was still a minor. The effect of this was to cause all the alliances across Europe to founder and a 17th century equivalent of World War I was averted. As for Henry, he died with his glory and reputation still intact. The dispute over the duchies of Cleves, Julich and Berg was settled amicably in 1614 through a compromise peace that could have been achieved in 1610 - but for an ageing King's lust for a young girl.

Duke of Buckingham

Buckingham, the most powerful man in England, was celebrating. He had just heard, wrongly as it turned out, that La Rochelle, the Protestant held French town which had been under siege by the Catholics for some months, had finally been relieved by the force he had sent to help.

Buckingham's good cheer, though, was short-lived. Later that very morning he was dead, stabbed through the heart by an assassin. As a result, thousands of other people were condemned to a similar fate, because the death of the noble duke was a contributory factor to the outbreak of the Civil War that rocked the kingdom in 1642.

The killer was John Felton, a member of the minor gentry, who had served as a lieutenant on a previous, also unsuccessful expedition to relieve La Rochelle. Felton was a sombre man, much given to reflection. He was also an angry and desperate man: angry at not getting the promotion he believed he had earned, and desperate because delays to a third planned expedition meant that he was not getting any pay.

And so he took it upon himself to rid the country of Buckingham, who, despite - or, more likely, because of - his power and influence was the most hated man in England. Member of Parliament, Sir John Eliot, talking of the damaging rift between Crown and Parliament, described him as '.... the cause of all our miseries.' Felton believed that killing him would be a service to the nation.

Buckingham totally dominated the government of the new king, Charles I. Indeed, Charles, a naturally timid man, was only too happy to let his friend run the country.

Unfortunately for Buckingham, however, he had made too many enemies in his life - and most MPs could be numbered among these.

Born on 28th August, 1592 in Leicestershire, George Villiers, as he was before becoming the first Duke of Buckingham, had enjoyed a rapid rise to fame and fortune. A bisexual, blessed with youthful good looks and charm, he became not only the favourite, but also the lover of King James I (1603-1625). However, his ambitions as a politician and statesman were to have a disastrous effect for himself and for the country.

Buckingham's unpopularity stemmed from his domination of first James and then Charles. His influence over these two kings was so overwhelming that they became merely a mouthpiece for his views. In addition, his attempts at foreign policy resembled pantomime farce.

In 1623 Europe was locked in combat in the Thirty Years War, and James was negotiating for a marriage alliance between the Infanta of Spain and Charles, the Prince of Wales. So eager were Charles and Buckingham to secure this alliance between Spain and England, that they made a mad dash through France to Spain, disguised in hoods and false beards and calling themselves Thomas and John Smith.

The plan backfired, however, when the pair were held as virtual hostages of the Spanish court. The whole enterprise became a humiliating failure and an embarrassment to England. The vain and overbearing duke's pride had suffered a blow, and he sought revenge. On returning home, he tried to persuade James to go to war with Spain. To this end, he instigated a raid on Cadiz in 1625. This adventure, however, far from emulating Sir Francis Drake's celebrated 'singeing of the King of Spain's beard,' turned into a fiasco.

Suffering from lack of water under the blazing sun, Buckingham's men could find only wine to slake their thirst. Before long they were drinking the King of Spain's health and raiding his wine stores rather than his fortresses.

It was small wonder, in the face of such damaging blows to England's prestige, that Buckingham became so unpopular with courtiers, politicians and the common people, or that his demise would be mourned by so few.

Death claimed him in the parlour of the Greyhound Inn at Portsmouth, where he had spent the night of 22nd August, 1625. The following morning, the duke was surrounded by a crowd, when John Felton suddenly jumped from the throng, plunging his dagger into his victim's breast.

Felton himself had fully expected to be cut down as soon as he had committed the deed, and had made no plans for a getaway. So he was surprised when, in the confusion, he was able to escape. The dying duke, blood gushing from his mouth, was laid on a table where his death was witnessed by his pregnant wife Kate, as she stood paralysed with horror in a gallery overlooking the hall.

Felton could have easily got away altogether - but for a misunderstanding. His pursuers, assuming the duke had been killed by an agent of Louis XIII of France, cried out: 'A Frenchman! A Frenchman!' Mishearing these cries and believing them to be calling his name, Felton gave himself up, saying: 'I am the man.'

He was sent to the Tower of London under arrest to await trial. On his way to London, however, he was fêted as a hero and national saviour by crowds lining his route - the David who slew a Goliath. But in prison, with time to reflect on what he had done, Felton came to believe that he had been guided by the Devil and not by God. So on 27th November he pleaded guilty to the charges brought against him and was sentenced to death. He was hanged on the 29th and his body was taken to Portsmouth where it was displayed in chains for all to see.

Few deaths can have been the cause of so much rejoicing as Buckingham's. Yet if he had lived, the course of history might have been very different. The Civil War between Parliament and the King might never have taken place, for it was Buckingham's domination of Charles in the early years of his reign that was the principal cause of the animosity between the King and Parliament.

From the outset it was because of Buckingham that Charles had failed to establish good relations with any of his parliaments; this, above all, lay at the heart of the outbreak of the war in 1642.

Nevertheless, while he lived, Buckingham had deflected the growing failures of the king onto himself and was a foil to Charles's growing unpopularity. While he lived, the rift between King and Parliament was never complete and possibly never would have been.

With Buckingham dead, however, there was no-one else to blame but the King. And slowly but surely the scene was set for the murderous butchery of England's most brutal and vicious period of strife.

Jean-Paul Marat

Who can doubt that, in late 18th century France, the King was corrupt and incompetent and his aristocratic henchmen downright despicable? Greedy, frivolous and indiscreet, their excesses, which had been a burden on France for years, did nothing to endear them to the ordinary working people. In their pampered, privileged worlds, they had no notion that the masses could rise up and oust them from their cosy palaces.

Rise up they did and the monarchy was toppled. Yet the rule of terror that replaced them was as bad, if not worse than the former royal regime. The blood-letting that took place cast a dark shadow over the new-found liberty of the people. As hysteria swept the streets, hundreds of people were killed without trial. At the heart of this shameful episode of French history was Jean-Paul Marat.

Marat was born in 1743, first son of a Swiss mother and a Spanish Calvinist father. His birthplace was Neuchatel, Switzerland, but he soon allied himself with neighbouring France. It was he who added the final 't' to his surname of Mara, in a bid to sound more like a native of the country he had adopted.

Marat travelled extensively in Holland, France and Britain, where he got a medical degree at St. Andrews, Scotland, and lent his support to British radical, John Wilkes. A thorn in the side of the out-of-touch British royals, Wilkes was an elected MP who was repeatedly expelled from the House of Commons for his outrageous behaviour and opposition to the monarchy.

Both Marat and Wilkes were advocates of a Bill of Rights in their respective countries - an act of Parliament which would curb the runaway powers of the monarchy and establish freedom of speech for the common man.

Marat returned to France, where his interest in politics far outweighed his commitment to medicine. In addition to a volley of vitriolic essays attacking the French King, Louis XVI, he launched a newspaper - first published only in Paris but then increasing its circulation throughout the whole of France - called *L'Ami Du Peuple* (Friend Of The People).

His patience with the dallying king, who, in the face of an economic calamity, introduced only the most half-hearted of reforms, quickly evaporated. Marat wasn't alone in his frustration. In 1789 the Bastille was stormed, the king was mobbed and a new parliament was installed.

Although the king reluctantly accepted the new French constitution, which introduced a bill of rights and abolished the feudalism which had operated in France, he remained unco-operative. The mood of the country was increasingly republican. The governing body, first called the Legislative Assembly and later known as the National Convention, became more extreme. Finally, the Convention declared France a republic. The King was executed on the guillotine in January, 1793, shortly before his queen, Marie Antoinette.

By the time the king lost his head Marat was already an established member of the Comité de Surveillance, the powerful body committed to rooting out opposition to the revolution. Often it was no better than a witch-hunt, pouncing on innocent families on the strength of a whispered accusation from a rival or mischief-maker.

The slaughter of an estimated 1,500 men, women and children in September, 1792 won Marat's backing. They were set upon in their cells or hauled out to face the guillotine in front of an angry mob, whipped into a frenzy by rumours that devious members of the nobility were about to undermine the revolution. None of those who died received a trial before being sentenced to death.

Marat's anger was inflamed by moderates, whom he saw as a danger to the success of the revolution. Marat became the bitterest enemy of the Girondins, a revolutionary force which was eminent in the Legislative Assembly. Their power base was in the Gironde region of France. But they had largely lost credibility due to their skirmishes with other European powers following the overthrow of Louis in 1789.

Marat aligned himself with the Jacobites, the more ruthless and ambitious arm of the revolution. Alongside Robespierre and Danton, he was one of their most forceful speakers. His squat figure rose up during stormy debates to issue a tirade of devastating blows. Once, he even threatened to shoot himself in the head if the Girondins acted against him. The crisis was averted, but Jacobites and Girondins continued to loathe each other.

Even after the death of the king, the Girondins were determined to gag the outspoken Marat. Examining his words in his newspaper, by now re-titled *Le Journal de la Republique Francaise* (The Journal of the French Republic), they believed that there was evidence enough to jail him for inciting murder and for his support of a dictatorship. As Marat was by now accomplished at manipulating the masses into a fervour and a long-time exponent of tyranny, there was certainly a strong element of truth in these accusations.

A revolutionary tribunal called to hear the accusations against Marat thought differently, however, and acquitted him within an hour. It was the end of the Girondins. Marat sought revenge by exiling some of those who had sided against him and executing others.

As he celebrated his victory, Marat had no idea that his days of rabble-rousing were drawing to a close. Just as he had flippantly determined the fate of so many, one woman had decided on his future with comparable callousness and determination.

Marie-Anne Charlotte Corday d'Armans was a native of Caen in Normandy, a stronghold of anti-Jacobite feeling. Like many others, she was horror-struck at the carnage on the streets of Paris. She heard one Girondist, Jeanne Pierre Brissot, denounce Marat as 'unfeeling, violent and cruel. Three hundred thousand heads must be struck off before liberty is established. That will be until this man Marat, whose soul is kneaded in blood and dirt, and is a disgrace to humanity and to the revolution, is dead.'

Aged 24, with a heart-shaped face and long, flowing hair, Charlotte Corday decided to become an assassin. She set off for Paris on 9th July, 1793 to seek out her quarry, leaving a note for her father, in which she begged him to forget her.

Contrary to her expectations, Marat was not at the Convention headquarters in the Tuileries. He suffered from a severe skin disorder which compelled him to take long and regular baths at his home. He claimed that the infection was contracted when he was forced to take refuge in the Paris sewers to escape the King's police before the revolution (although nowadays it is thought that the condition was probably advanced herpes). So Corday went to his house and pleaded to be allowed in.

Twice she was turned away until she finally persuaded Marat's sister and mistress to grant her an audience. She had, she confided, valuable information about subversives in the north of the country which could be vital to the security of the revolution.

When Corday entered his room, Marat was soaking in the bath, where he composed death lists and newspaper articles. As she began imparting her information, he responded with alacrity: 'I shall send them all to the guillotine in a few days,' he announced.

With that Corday ripped from her blouse the butcher's knife she had bought for two francs only days earlier, and plunged it into his chest. The deep wound pierced his lung and heart. As blood flooded into the bathwater, Marat called for his mistress. She barely made it to his side before he died.

Corday attempted to walk from the scene but was tackled by Marat's staff. As they led her away raining blows on her, she cried 'I don't care. The deed is done - the monster is dead.'

Swiftly put before a tribunal, she declared that she had nothing to say: 'Nothing, except that I have succeeded.'

Marat's body lay in state for two days, during which hundreds paid homage to him. He was elevated to the ranks of people's martyr instead of being unmasked as the blood-thirsty maniac that he was.

Four days after the killing, Corday was guillotined. She died never knowing that her act triggered off another wave of murder and mayhem directed at the country's ill-starred aristocracy. The Reign of Terror operated by the leaders of the revolution continued unabated until the execution of another of them, Robespierre.

Spencer Perceval

Nothing about the Right Honourable Spencer Perceval was as memorable as his death. As a man, he was an unknown; as a politician, he was riding a fast horse to obscurity. Even the office of Prime Minister was obtained only because the Tory party could not agree on a suitable successor to the Duke of Portland, who resigned on health grounds in 1809.

Only one thing has ensured that the name of Spencer Perceval was never forgotten: he was the only British Prime Minister to be assassinated.

His killer, John Bellingham, was a typical entrepreneur of the day who had built up a sizeable international business with large interests in Russia. Unfortunately for him, in 1811 he fell foul of the Tsarist police and was imprisoned. As a consequence, he lost both his business and his personal fortune.

On his release, Bellingham complained about his treatment to the British Consul General in St. Petersburg. But for some reason this official either could not or would not help. Bellingham returned home a bitter and angry man. He took his case to his MP. However, dissatisfied with this man's efforts - or lack of them - he deluged other politicians and the Prime Minister himself with letters demanding hard action against the Russian authorities.

The answer was always the same. In the opinion of the British authorities, Bellingham had earned his time in jail for failing to observe Russian laws. Bellingham decided on the ultimate protest: he would gun down the man who symbolised the establishment that had refused to help him.

So, on 11th May, 1812 Bellingham was waiting in the

crowded lobby of the House of Commons when the small, wiry figure of Spencer Perceval hurried in from nearby Downing Street and turned to go to the Chamber. Suddenly Bellingham stepped from behind a pillar and raised a pistol. He fired, and from point-blank range hit the Prime Minister full in the chest.

Perceval was carried quickly to the Speaker's chambers but died before a doctor could reach him. Outside in the lobby, pandemonium reigned. In the midst of the panic, a voice boomed: 'Who is the villain who fired?'

Bellingham, resplendent in a brightly coloured coat with metal buttons, replied: 'I am that unfortunate man,' whereupon he was marched off to the cells below the Palace of Westminster. So the politician who had hitherto been notable only for his mediocrity finally had fame thrust upon him.

As for Bellingham, a number of conspiracy theories were put about on the strength of his name being Anglo-Irish. But he himself put a stop to these with the declaration: 'It is a private injury.'

There was one more incident of note that emerged from the affair. It was clear that Bellingham was unbalanced, and in court his lawyer, Sir James Mansfield, argued for the first time that the criterion for criminal responsibility in mental cases should be whether the accused had a sufficient degree of intellectual capacity to distinguish between good and evil at the time of committing the offence.

The argument was accepted and thirty years later it became part of English law. But it did not help John Bellingham. His plea of insanity was not accepted by the court and on 18th May, 1812 he was hanged at Newgate Prison behind London's Old Bailey courtroom.

Abraham Lincoln

For many months President Abraham Lincoln had been haunted by a disturbing nightmare. In it he found himself wandering aimlessly through the corridors of the White House as though searching for an elusive goal. The dream ended when he entered a room and discovered his own body.

The experience was not something Lincoln had discussed, except with his wife. Perhaps he put it down to the stress he had been suffering through the final months of the bloody American Civil War. As spring arrived in 1865 he felt like a man drained of strength and spirit; a man in need of weeks of sleep and rejuvenation.

On 14th April Lincoln sat at his presidential desk in Washington DC contemplating the task of reuniting America. As victor and head of the Yankee forces he knew he was a figure of hate in the vanquished Southern states. In the four years since he'd been sworn in as First Citizen - a term of office which almost exactly coincided with the length of the Civil War - he had been the target of no fewer than eighty-two separate assassination plots. One, in 1862, was literally a whisker away from success. Then a bullet had passed through his stove-pipe hat but miraculously failed to draw blood.

Throughout this trial of personal courage, Lincoln had maintained his dignity and common sense. He even told the *Washington Chronicle*: 'The only certain way to eliminate all risk to the person of the President is to imprison him in an iron box where he cannot be made a target for assassins and he cannot perform his duties for the Union.'

On that April day, the President was feeling as weary

Abraham Lincoln: The US President was shot at the theatre.

as ever. The war had effectively ended just five days earlier when the leading Southern general, Robert E. Lee, surrendered the remains of his northern Virginia army to General Ulysses S. Grant at the Appomattox Court House in Virginia. Now the task had begun of healing wounds and soothing bitter hatreds. Lincoln was a man open to ideas as he chaired his cabinet meeting at 11 am.

When the meeting broke up, however, he turned his mind to other matters. He and his wife were expected to attend a performance of Tom Taylor's comedy *Our American Cousin*, starring Laura Keane, at the Ford Theatre that night. He wondered whether the Grants would like to join them? It was to be the President's first public appearance since the end of the war and it would surely be fitting for the general, a hero of the Union cause, to be at his side.

The general offered his apologies but had to decline. He was expected back in New Jersey that evening for what would be an emotional reunion with his sons. Little did he know that his determination to keep that promise was to save his life.

Lincoln tried in vain to persuade other senior Cabinet colleagues to join him. But when Secretary of State Stanton also refused, on the unequivocal grounds that he hated the theatre, the President was resigned to fulfil his important engagement with only some junior aides and a bodyguard. In the end it was a young army major, Henry Rathbone, and his fiancée, Clara Harris, who stepped into the theatre's Presidential box with the Lincolns.

The theatre visit was public knowledge and had not escaped the attention of Lincoln's enemies in the South. Chief among these turned out to be the actor, John Wilkes Booth, a man who regarded Lincoln as the Devil incarnate. Not only did Booth want revenge for the humiliation of the Southern forces, but he also feared the effects of Lincoln's plan to abolish slavery. Booth also nurtured a massive chip on his shoulder. He had never plucked up the courage to actually fight for the South; now perhaps he could make amends by disposing of Lincoln.

Booth, a lanky man with a pallid complexion and flowing black locks, had already cooked up one plan to kidnap Lincoln in late 1864. The theory was that, by holding the President as a bargaining chip, the Unionists would have to negotiate a truce on terms favoured by the South. Twice Booth and his fellow plotters set a date to strike, only for the President to change his plans at the last minute. Then the war suddenly ended and revenge became John Booth's prime motive.

It was early afternoon on 14th April when he convened a meeting of the conspirators at the Washington boarding house of Mary Surratt on 'H' Street. The others present were George A. Atzerodt, Sam Arnold, David Herold and Lewis Paine. Their deliberations were heavily fuelled by drink, but once it became clear that they were serious about an attempt on the life of the President and other senior government figures, Arnold stormed out. He declared that he would have no truck with murder. The rest agreed that later that evening Paine should kill Secretary of State William H. Seward, Atzerodt would murder Vice President Andrew Johnston and Booth himself would target Lincoln.

The President arrived at the Ford Theatre just after 8 pm. The performance had already started but it was halted almost as soon as he stepped into the auditorium. The orchestra played *Hail to the Chief* and the audience of two thousand stood and cheered the man whom they regarded as America's saviour.

Lincoln was shown to his private box and guided to a rocking chair set a little back from the edge of the balcony. He was grateful. The chair would allow him to doze a little during the performance without any risk of showing his countrymen just how weary he had become.

Booth, meanwhile, timed his arrival at the theatre for 9.30 pm. He had done his groundwork well in advance, having recently played in a production at Fords, and knew many of the stagehands by name. He had even sneaked in earlier in the day to plan his strategy and noted that the lock on the door of the Presidential box did not function properly. He drilled a spy-hole, giving him a perfect view of the rocking chair allocated to the President. He also secreted a plank of wood which he would use to jam the door behind him.

Booth knew the play well and he had worked out that certain lines spoken by the character Brother Jonathan (whose flowing beard would later become the model for Uncle Sam) were certain to bring the house down. That would be the moment to fire on Lincoln. Silently he walked to the door of the box, fully prepared to knock the President's personal guard, John Parker, unconscious. But Parker was not at his post. He had made the assassination unbelievably simple by wandering off for a drink at a convenient local bar.

At about 10.15 pm, Booth stormed into the box and, mouthing the Latin phrase 'Sic semper tyrannis' (thus ever to tyrants), he squeezed the trigger of his six inch Derringer pistol.

It sent a 7/16 lead ball into the back of Lincoln's skull, searing into his brain above his left ear. The bullet came to a halt behind the right eye of the President, who slumped forward in his chair.

Instantly, Major Rathbone attacked Booth, who responded by pulling a knife and slashing the officer's arm. The assassin then leapt onto the stage, twisting his riding spur in curtains as he fell, and landed awkwardly breaking his leg. As the theatre heaved with a panicked and confused audience, he managed to push a few people out of his path and escaped limping to his horse and the safety of the night.

Lincoln was lifted - still in his chair - to a nearby boarding house in Tenth Street. He remained alive, fighting for his life, for several hours, but it was clear to all who saw him that his time was up.

The premonition of death he had seen in his dreams was fulfilled and at 7.22 am the following day the Surgeon General, Dr. Robert Stone, pronounced him dead. Those present later told how his face seemed to settle into Lincoln's first peaceful expression in four years. Silver dollars were gently placed over his eyes and Secretary of State Stanton murmured a simple tribute: 'Now, he belongs to the ages.'

The other two assassins had been unable to match Booth's success. Though Lewis Paine had managed to break into Seward's house, and stab the old fellow with a dagger, the wound was far from fatal. As for Atzerodt, he lost his nerve and went off to get drunk.

Eleven days later, Booth and Herold were hunted down to their bolthole: an old tobacco barn near Fort Royal, Virginia. Soldiers failed to persuade them to surrender and so the order was given to torch the barn. Herold gave himself up, but, as the heat became unbearable, Booth shot himself.

For the rest of the conspirators, time was also running

out. On 7th July, 1865 Paine, Herold, Atzerodt and Mrs Surratt (whose only crime appears to be that she had the misfortune to own the boarding house where the plot was hatched) were all executed by hanging. Others who played a lesser role in the conspiracy were sentenced to long years of hard labour.

John Booth's actions may have given him personal satisfaction. But they did little for his fellow southerners. Infuriated at the assassination plot, right-wing Republicans demanded reprisals against the South and new President Andrew Johnson found himself steamrollered into meeting many of their demands. It was not how Abraham Lincoln would have wished it. Arguably, his death set back the cause of civil rights in America a hundred years.

Lincoln's funeral train took twelve days to steam from Washington to Springfield, Illinois, where he was at last laid to rest in Oakridge cemetery.

Tsar Alexander II

The killing of Tsar Alexander II of Russia was one of the great tragic acts of modern history. For the death of this progressive and reforming monarch led to a period of repression and reaction that culminated in the Russian Revolution, the Cold War and the misery that remains today after the dissolution of the Soviet Empire.

Alexander succeeded to the throne in March, 1855 at the age of 36. Russia was fighting the French and the British in the Crimea, but was in no state to continue, being bankrupt both politically and financially. Alexander saw the need for change and negotiated the Treaty of Paris in 1856.

He was no liberal - rather a pragmatic conservative, who saw that the monarchy would survive only if there were reform brought in from above. His most progressive act was the freeing of the serfs in 1861. At a stroke twenty-three million slaves became free men. Reform also came in local government, the army and the legal system, where trial by jury was instituted.

Ironically, the result of such changes was that in the more liberal political climate former slaves demanded ever greater reforms. There was an uprising in Poland and terrorism increased, some of it directed against the Tsar. Such pressure forced Alexander to abandon his policies temporarily and adopt stern measures. Reactionaries were appointed to the government in a bid to quell the unrest.

The result, however, was that the insurrectionists became even more determined - until finally the Tsar saw that the only way out was to complete his reforms package, while at the same time cracking down on the revolutionaries.

Alexander led a charmed life. There were repeated attempts on his life that came to nothing. In 1861 a man fired a pistol into his coach, but, even at point blank range, missed the Tsar. Police uncovered two plots against his life in the following two years. And in 1866 a pistol wielding student was jostled in the street just as he was taking aim at the Tsar.

In 1879, while Alexander was out walking, he noticed a man acting suspiciously. The ruler was quick-witted enough to get out of the way as the man drew a pistol and fired three times before fleeing. The would-be assassin was brought to a halt by a milkwoman before being overpowered by the crowd.

Later that year there were two attempts to blow up the Tsar's train as he travelled home from the Crimea; one by the terrorist, Zhelyabov, the other by Alexander's mistress, Sophia Perovsky.

Zhelyabov made it his life's work to kill the Tsar, organising numerous other attempts and in 1880 providing the dynamite for another plotter to blow up the Winter Palace.

This was the nearest that the plotters got to success. A bomb was set on a timing device to go off during a banquet. Luckily for Alexander, he had remained in his study, waiting for his son to arrive.

Many innocents were slaughtered in the bomb attempt, as they were in Perovsky's attempt on the royal train. Her mistake was to dynamite the wrong train, and hundreds perished while the target was miles away.

At this stage the Tsar blundered. Instead of executing Sophia Perovsky, he gave her money to go to America, where she continued plotting. Eventually she joined forces with Zhelyabov to organise the successful attempt on her former lover's life.

On the day of Alexander's death, 14th March, 1881, the Tsar had signed a new constitution that allowed the people representation in central government, something they had always been denied. His interior minister was aware that an assassination attempt was to be made, and urged the Tsar not to attend the usual parade of guards.

In fact Zhelyabov and Perovsky had already mined a number of streets through which the royal party was likely to pass. Zhelyabov was arrested on 13th March, but he refused to talk. Alexander decided to ignore the advice of his interior minister and drove into St. Petersburg. It was his second tragic error.

His first call was to see the Grand Duchess Catherine. As he returned to his coach, a man called Rysakov hurled a nitroglycerine bomb, but, miscalculating the distance, ended up killing a number of the Tsar's Cossack escort. It seemed as if Alexander had escaped again.

But here the monarch made his third and final error. Instead of fleeing to safety, as his coachman suggested, Alexander turned to see to the welfare of his men. This gave another member of the gang, Grinevetskii, the opportunity to throw a second bomb at the Tsar's feet. The blast struck down both victim and assassin, blowing away one of Alexander's legs and shattering the other to the top of the thigh. The Tsar lay in a pool of his own blood before being taken to his palace, where he died within the hour. The terrorists had got what they wanted, but the consequences were terrible for Russia and all the citizens of the empire.

In response to his father's violent end the new Tsar, Alexander III, abandoned all thoughts of reform and ushered in a new dark age of autocratic repression. Russia again became stagnant at a time when she could have become a great modern power alongside Britain, France and Germany. Harshest of all was the inevitable slide to the 1917 revolution that engulfed Russia in misery and hardship - and the rise of Communism, which gripped the Soviet Union for seventy dark years.

James A. Garfield

In his mind, Charles J. Guiteau had played a vital role in the successful 1880 election campaign of United States President James A. Garfield. Guiteau had written a rallying speech which he thought potent enough to sway the nation. His reward, he believed, would be the plum job of ambassador to France. He would settle for nothing less.

In reality, Guiteau was a sad figure who bored anyone he met so acutely that they ignored him ever after. The speech which he had so painstakingly composed went unheard. While a few politicians sympathised with his theories, none of them was prepared to legitimise his effort to gatecrash the political scene. Even Guiteau himself failed to deliver his 'masterpiece'. He attempted to do so only once, at a black rally in New York. Within moments, the tiny audience dwindled to nothing. A lonely Guiteau abandoned the rostrum and went home.

President Garfield, troubled by the splintering of his own Republican Party, paid scant attention to Guiteau's repeated requests for a job and therefore never realised how much the mind of this persistent lawyer-cum-evangelist had been twisted by his urge to be famous. Sadly, this oversight cost Garfield his life.

It would have taken little probing to discover that Guiteau was probably insane. His father, Luther Guiteau, was known to be at best eccentric, at worst quite mad. An uncle and two cousins ended up in an asylum and two aunts were deemed to be of unsound mind.

Guiteau was born on 8th September, 1841 into a family committed to the fringe Oneida Community. Based outside New York, it not only expounded unorthodox religious views, in particular proclaiming that Jesus had been reborn in the first century, but also believed in free love for its members. He grew up to be an active supporter of this unusual group, extracting finance from it for a trip to New York and Chicago to further his embryonic career as a newspaperman. The bid to enter print journalism failed and instead he became a lawyer.

In Chicago he met and married teenager, Annie Bunn, and they spent five years living hand-to-mouth around the city. In 1874, Annie divorced him on the grounds of adultery. Guiteau freely admitted that he regularly visited prostitutes and that he had contracted syphilis from one of them.

His next project was a book called *The Truth: A Companion to The Bible* - its avowed aim not to make money but to save souls. Without the notoriety he was to gain as the assassin of the president, this weighty tome would doubtless have sunk without trace.

After that came an abiding passion in politics. At first Guiteau flirted with the Democrats, angling for the post of Minister to Chile with Horace Greely's camp. Eight years later he hitched himself to the Republican bandwagon, in which he was markedly more successful. It was for the 1880 elections that he penned the speech he considered to be so significant, entitled 'Garfield vs Hancock' (the Democratic nominee). It was largely a rant against the Confederate states of America, newly incorporated in the Union. He had it printed at his own expense and distributed it to key figures in the campaign.

Garfield, a general for the Union in the American Civil War, was an 11th hour compromise candidate, whose task was to bridge the factions of his own party, profoundly split on the way forward. One side, called the Stalwarts, were opposed to reform in the Civil Service and harboured a grudge against the states of the the Confederacy. The other was known as the Half-Breeds, boasting a more liberal outlook. Garfield favoured the latter.

Guiteau now had his sights set on a post in Paris. Week in, week out, Guiteau continued his lobbying at the White House for the French post which he believed he richly deserved. Nothing happened. He was soon to be barred from the White House and was so much of a nuisance that Secretary of State James Blaine once rounded on him, yelling 'Never speak to me again about the Paris consulship as long as you live!'

Meanwhile, the cracks in the Republican Party grew deeper and more crucial. The embittered Guiteau sided with disconsolate right-wingers. It dawned on him that he was a man with a mission. His mission was to kill the President and save the country.

In June 1881, he bought himself a bone-handled .44 calibre revolver and put in some shooting practice along the banks of the Potomac river. Soon he was ready to tackle his target.

Even though it was only sixteen years since the assassination of President Abraham Lincoln, security around Garfield was woefully sparse. If he was not sure of the movements of the President, Guiteau simply checked with the doorman of the White House, who would happily confirm Garfield's plans.

His first chance came soon enough when Garfield visited a church. However, Guiteau decided against pulling the trigger at the sight of Garfield's wife at his side. It was a few weeks before fate once again put Guiteau in the same room as the unsuspecting Garfield. The president was setting off on holiday, leaving via the Baltimore & Potomac railway station. Accompanied by Blaine, he embarked from his official carriage and entered the station through the ladies' waiting room. Lurking in the corner was the sinister figure of Guiteau, clad in black from head to toe.

When the President was only a few feet away, Guiteau produced his gun and shot Garfield in the back. As he collapsed in agony, Garfield cried 'My God, what is this?' Not content with causing a gaping wound, Guiteau blasted the revolver at Garfield again, this time missing completely.

A policeman felled Guiteau as he made a half-hearted attempt to escape. His words to the shocked officer were: 'It's all right. Keep quiet, my friend. I wish to go to jail. Now Arthur (successor President Chester Arthur) is President of the United States. I am a Stalwart of Stalwarts.' In his hand was a note for General William Sherman asking for military protection from a vengeful crowd.

Despite the damage done to his backbone and a major artery, the President initally survived the attack. He faced a series of crises from which he stabilised only to fall seriously ill once more. Anxious hordes gathered around public billboards which gave updates on his health. At one stage, Garfield was well enough to resume some minor presidential duties. It was two months before the injury finally claimed his life.

A tumultuous trial began in November, 1881 with Guiteau indulging in some theatrical outbursts. He branded witnesses 'dirty liars' and the prosecutor 'a low-livered whelp' or 'old hog'. He insisted that he had acted on God's orders and advised the jury: 'Let your verdict be that it was the Deity's act, not mine.' When the defence claims of insanity were dismissed by the jury and he was found guilty of murder, he waggled a finger at the jurors and uttered: 'You are all low, consummate jackasses.'

Guiteau himself was the target of two assassination attempts while behind bars, both of which failed. While in jail, he suggested a monument to himself should be erected with the inscription: 'Here lies the body of Charles Guiteau, patriot and Christian. His soul is in glory.'

His execution by hanging was scheduled for 30th June, 1882, almost a year to the day since the attack. Thousands flocked to the prison. Guiteau used the grim occasion finally to recite a piece of his own work to an audience. The poem he wrote for the event went like this:

'I am going to the Lordy; I am so glad. I am going to the Lordy; I am so glad. I am going to the Lordy, Glory Hallelujah! Glory Hallelujah! I am going to the Lordy I wonder what I will do when I get to the Lordy? I guess that I will weep no more when I get to the Lordy. Glory Hallelujah! I wonder what I will see when I get to the Lordy? I expect to see most splendid things beyond all earthly conception when I am with the Lordy, Glory Hallelujah.'

The last words heard by the mystified crowd inside the prison courtyard before the trap door opened were: 'Glory, glory, glory.'

William McKinley

At the turn of the century the world's democracies were on their guard against a reborn creed that seemed to be spreading uncontrollably. It was called anarchism and it appealed to the young and the idealistic, as well as to the totally deranged.

This idea was nothing new. It dated back three hundred years before the birth of Christ to the time of the Greek philosopher, Zeno of Citium. Yet it was the way anarchy was now being interpreted that caused rulers and politicians so much concern for the future of democratic society. Anarchists were arguing that there could be no freedom while a government laid down rules. The only path to a truly free world, they insisted, was for the state to be dismantled and replaced with a series of open agreements between individuals over the way life should be lived.

For hundreds of years discussion of anarchism had been confined largely to intellectuals and philosophers. Its rebirth in Russia towards the end of the 19th century, when it was deployed as a doctrine of violence, did not go un-noticed in the West, however. By the time anarchists assassinated King Humbert I at Monza, Italy, in 1905, many politicians were warning of an anarchic plot to destabilise the free world.

Nowhere did the rumours acquire more currency than in the United States of America, where followers of the unpredictable new movement were regarded by politicians as the enemy within. High on the list of demagogues was an earnest young woman called Emma Goldman, whose impassioned speeches calling for the overthrow of governments quickly won her a small army of fanatical followers. In 1901 one of those followers was Leon Czolgosz (pronounced 'Colgosh'), who decided it was his destiny to strike for the cause. His target, he decided, would be President William McKinley.

McKinley, a staunch Republican and veteran of the Union Army during the Civil War, was elected in 1896. Backed by the wealthy Ohio politician, Marcus A. Hanna, he ran on a cornerstone policy of support for the gold standard, combined with rigorous protectionist tarifs against imported goods. He was a popular leader, not least for the way he was perceived to have given the US its first major voice in world affairs. It was McKinley who took his country into the Spanish American War and who would later take the credit for winning control of the Philippines, Hawaii and Cuba. Good relations with China enhanced his reputation as a conservative with innovative ideas.

McKinley was, of course, aware that anarchism had reared its head in America, but didn't regard it with any great concern. Democracy, he reasoned, was nothing if it could not withstand bizarre and outspoken viewpoints. He regarded press stories of an anarchist-inspired master plan to kill world leaders with equanimity. Emma Goldman and her followers gave him no cause for concern and he dismissed pleas by his worried aides to become more security conscious. 'Last year it was Humbert, you're the next obvious target,' they warned him.

At the end of August the rumour-mill was churning out tittle-tattle on the anarchist 'subversives' at a furious rate. So much so, that the President's secretary, George Cortelyou, tried to talk McKinley out of attending a very public reception at the Pan American Exposition in Buffalo, New York State.

'Just give the speech, Sir,' Cortelyou pleaded, 'you can easily cancel the reception.' McKinley simply shrugged and replied 'Why should I. No-one would wish to hurt me.' Despite the President's calm approach, his dutiful secretary decided to take no chances. At least fifty security guards and secret service agents were detailed to protect him during the Buffalo visit.

Leon Czolgosz, meanwhile, had booked himself into a small doss-house room above a saloon in Buffalo. On Tuesday, 3rd September, 1901 he purchased a highly distinctive .32 calibre Iver Johnson pistol, complete with owl-head motif stamped onto the handle. He practised handling and firing it and then formulated a plan to assassinate the President as he left his private rail coach inside the exposition area.

That day he was frustrated. The police cordon held sightseers so far back that it would have been impossible to squeeze off a reliable shot. The following day McKinley addressed a crowd in which Czolgosz was lurking. Again the gunman found he was too far away to risk an attack.

The assassin decided that there would be no harm in stalking the President a little longer, and within twenty-four hours he was mingling with crowds at the Temple of Music, a magnificent, ornate, octagonal building at the centre of the exposition. Sure enough the President arrived on schedule at the Temple, and at 4 pm the doors were opened to allow the public to get close to their First Citizen. Czolgosz was in the initial surge of people through the door and he took up position in a queue of excited hand-shakers. His pistol was wrapped in a white bandage - it looked as though he'd burned himself, as secret service agent Sam Ireland recalled later - but nothing else about Czolgosz seemed at all unusual. Besides, the security men had other things on their mind. The weather was unbearably hot and humid and many of them were looking forward to a break.

Czolgosz's queue inched towards the nodding, smiling President as he stood on a raised dais. To one side stood John Milburn, the president of the Exposition and fanning around the two men the secret service agents cast an eye over the crowd. As Czolgosz's turn to meet McKinley arrived, Sam Ireland placed his hand on the assassin's shoulder, planning to steady him and move him forward as quickly as possible once the handshake was over.

The handshake never came. The President produced his automatic politician's smile and extended his hand but Czolgosz thrust it aside as he levelled the concealed pistol. The gun spat twice, hitting McKinley once in the chest and once in the stomach.

As the President lurched back into a chair, his face deathly pale, eight agents pounced on Czolgosz, forcing him to the ground. One grabbed the gun, burning his hand on the flaming bandage. Others hauled him to his feet, their contorted faces expressing a mixture of panic and fury, and began beating him with fists and rifle butts. One guard with a fixed bayonet seemed ready to finish off the killer there and then. Only a gasped order from the President held the trooper back: 'Be easy with him, boys.'

The crowd was not so easily placated. Some people followed secret service men into a secluded room a few yards away and helped them to carry out a brutal beating on the assassin. One, a waiter called James Parker, recalled later 'We thumped him and slapped his face. I took a knife out of my pocket and started to cut his throat, but he never flinched. Gamest man I ever saw in my life.'

Eventually police heaved Czolgosz's battered body

from the table where he lay and sped him downtown to police headquarters. There it was their turn to interrogate him 'to the third degree', even though their prisoner was willing to confess his guilt.

The President, meanwhile, had been taken to the Exposition's on-site hospital where surgeons performed an exploratory operation. It was clear that the chest wound was largely superficial and would have healed. But the shot through the stomach had caused far more serious damage. The doctors decided that there was no chance of finding the bullet, which they suspected was lodged near the spine. There was little alternative but to sew up the wound and hope for the best. McKinley was taken to the home of his friend, John Milburn, to rest and the nation waited anxiously for bulletins on his condition.

At first the news was up-beat. The President had taken food and drink and even asked for a cigar, a request his doctors had denied. The day after the attack the *New York Times* comforted its readers with the words: 'All the official bulletins showed great gains and inspired those near the President to state positively that he would recover rapidly. The strain on the heart-strings of the nation has been relieved.'

It was a false hope. Shortly after 2 am on 14th September McKinley's condition took a sudden turn for the worse. By evening there seemed little doubt that he was close to death and at 7 am he asked for his wife - herself physically and emotionally drained - to come to his bedside to spend some time with him. She was still there at 2 am the following morning to hear him murmur a few lines from the hymn *Nearer My God To Thee*.

His last words were: 'Goodbye all. Goodbye. It is God's way. His will be done.' By 2.15 it was over. The post-mortem examination revealed the cause of death as gangrene poisoning.

At 7.12 am on 20th October in Auburn, New York, Leon Czolgosz was executed in the electric chair. He had been tried and found guilty and never once showed a hint of remorse. Czolgosz's last words as he was strapped into the electric chair were: 'I killed the President because he was the enemy of the good people - the good working people. I am not sorry for my crime.' Half a minute later the switch was thrown and officials erased all trace of Czolgosz's body by pouring sulphuric acid over it after it was placed in the grave.

However, Czolgosz left behind him a legacy of fear and suspicion across America; many who dared to speak out against the government were wrongly labelled as anarchists. One brave individual who publicly voiced sympathy for Czolgosz in Casper, Wyoming, found himself tarred and feathered and run out of town.

It would be left to Vice President Theodore Roosevelt to try to calm the nation. In part he succeeded, his more liberal policies finding favour with many voters. But for a long time in the 'land of the free' anarchy was to remain a symbol of terrorism to be exposed and destroyed at every opportunity.

Archduke
Francis Ferdinand

It was over in a flash. Two shots fired from a crowd and the man poised to become one of Europe's most powerful tyrants fell down dead in an open car.

Yet the repercussions of those brief moments of anarchy echoed around the world for years. The shots turned out to be the opening volley of World War I, which cost millions of lives. Even the peace deal which eventually ended the carnage sowed the seeds for another devastating international conflict, World War II, which erupted within twenty years.

It was the summer of 1914 when the assassin struck, unknowingly shaping world history by his act. He was Gavrilo Princip, a 19-year-old Serbian revolutionary who yearned for independence for his homeland. The target was Archduke Francis Ferdinand, the portly heir to the throne of the massive, powerful Austro-Hungarian empire.

Ferdinand was set to take power on the death of his uncle, Emperor Francis Joseph, an ailing old man of 83, who had held the reins of power since the age of 18. But the unwieldy kingdom was not a happy one. It was made up of Austria and Hungary, united by an uneasy alliance since 1867, and included eleven other nationalities, among them Czechs, Serbs and Croats.

The region had been shaken by the ferocity of the recent Balkan Wars between the various ambitious factions. Resentment was festering once more. Emperor Francis Joseph was wearied by a succession of personal tragedies. His brother, Maximillian, had been executed in

The two shots in Sarajevo in June, 1914, which led to the deaths of 10 million men in World War I.

Mexico, his son, Rudolf, committed suicide and his wife, Elisabeth, was murdered by revolutionaries. But he continued to rule with an iron fist, abhorring democracy.

His nephew was arguably more progressive. However, he had married the woman he loved, the Countess Sophie Chotek, a Czech of low nobility, and therefore tended to favour the case of her people above those of the other nationalities in the Austro-Hungarian Empire. So controversial was the marriage, that Ferdinand had to sign away the rights of their children to the throne of the empire. It certainly soured relations between the Archduke and his uncle.

Princip was one of many young men who believed passionately in a brighter future for his fellow Serbs. He was born in 1895, the son of a peasant farmer on the Bosnian-Dalmatian border. Attractive, with clear, sallow skin, black hair and bright blue eyes, Princip could easily have found himself romance and fun. Not for him, however, were the delights of drinking and dancing.

The serious-minded youngster concentrated instead on literature and the study of revolutionary ideals. He was a member of the nationalist group 'Mlada Bosna' or 'Young Bosnia' and devoted all his spare time and energy to the movement. When he heard that the Archduke was to visit the Bosnian city of Sarajevo, the disgruntled student pledged to kill him.

For assistance he turned to the thriving secret society run by Serb army officers known as 'The Black Hand'. Its motto was 'Death or Unity' and its aim was to reunite all Serbs living under Austrian and Turkish dominance in a land of their own. It was instrumental not only in training Princip and a handful of accomplices but also in providing ammunition.

The Archduke was aware of the dangers involved in his state visit to Bosnia as Inspector General to the empire's armed forces. He was warned of assassination plots, but dismissed them out of hand.

He and his wife were travelling in a royal motorcade on the morning of 28th June, 1914. Unusually for a royal visit, there were no soldiers lining the streets, despite the mounting ill feeling towards the dignitary. So lax was the security, that few police were in evidence on the route. The royal pair progressed slowly along Appel Quai, a smart boulevard which ran alongside the River Miljacka, waving at the crowd, which was, for the most part, enthusiastic.

Without warning, a missile came flying through the air towards the car. It was a bomb thrown by another anarchist, Nedeljko Cabrinovic, and it was large enough to cause extensive damage. Some reports claim that the bomb bounced off the canvas canopy on the car, others that the Archduke himself picked it up and hurled it away. In any event, it exploded on the road beneath the wheels of another vehicle in the procession, causing injury to both occupants and bystanders.

Coolly, the royal pair decided to continue on to a civic reception as planned. Cabrinovic, meanwhile, had popped a cyanide capsule into his mouth - the hallmark of a Black Hand activist - and dived into the river to escape capture. The water made him sick and, after vomiting the poison, he was detained by police.

At the town hall the mayor, apparently unaware of the assassination attempt, delivered his welcome speech with fervour. The Archduke answered gruffly: 'We come to Sarajevo, Herr Burgermeister, and have a bomb thrown at us.'

Archduke Ferdinand was doubtless congratulating

himself on his narrow escape. Little did he know that there were no less than six other potential assassins on the streets of Sarajevo hoping to succeed where Cabrinovic had failed.

On the return journey, these six appeared to lose heart for their grisly task or simply did not have the opportunity. Princip himself didn't recognise the Archduke as he proceeded back down Appel Quai and retired in disgust to a café to brood on his bad luck.

Then fate took a hand. The procession made an unscheduled turn into Franz Joseph Street. In the confusion, it ground to a halt just outside the café where Princip was consoling himself with a coffee.

He wasn't going to fail a second time. In a flash, he produced the Browning revolver from his pocket and blasted off two bullets. One hit Countess Sophie in the stomach as she threw herself in the line of fire to defend her husband; the other pierced the 51-year-old Archduke's jugular vein, splattering his smart military uniform with blood.

He turned to his beloved wife to plead with her: 'Soferl, Soferl, don't die. Live for my children.' But it was too late. She already lay dead from her gaping wound. And the Archduke collapsed and died ten minutes later amid the chaos caused by the shots.

There was uproar in Sarajevo at their deaths. Outraged authorities rounded up dozens of young men whom they believed might be responsible for the crimes, Princip among them. Suspected conspirators were brutally treated by police. Several were sentenced to death. Princip was given twenty years hard labour. He lived to see the effect of his drastic actions from a harsh prison camp in Austria before succumbing to the ravages of tuberculosis in 1918.

The shockwaves from the killing were immediately felt world-wide. In London, *The Times* said: 'It shakes the conscience of the world.' With foresight *The Daily Chronicle* spoke of a 'clap of thunder' over Europe.

In Austria the horror and indignation fuelled anti-Serbian demonstrations, at which the national Serbian flag was burnt. The people bayed for reprisals.

Meanwhile, in Serbian Belgrade there was little attempt to hide the smugness and satisfaction which both the government and people felt at the news.

Austrians were convinced that the Serbian government was involved in the plot. In fact, the government and the Black Hand were frequently at odds and were unlikely bedfellows. Nevertheless, the Austrians gave Serbia an ultimatum. If they wanted to avoid war, the government had to undertake to smash the Black Hand, put an end to the black propaganda against Austria and allow Austrian police into Serbia to root out guilty activists.

Clearly, Serbia could not accept these terms in full, and Austria did not really expect the little country to do so. For Austria was determined to exact revenge through open warfare and, ultimately, to destroy the 'hornet's nest' with old ally Germany at its side.

But Serbia had powerful friends too, in the form of Russia, which could count Britain, France and the low countries as its allies.

On 28th July, 1914 Austro-Hungary declared war on Serbia. The following day Russia mobilised its forces along its borders with Germany and Austria. On 1st August Germany declared war on Russia and, days later, on France and Belgium. Britain had long been irritated at the naval rivalry and muscle-flexing displayed by Germany. Prime Minister Herbert Asquith made his declaration of war on Germany to cheers in the House of Commons on 4th August.

Germany and Austro-Hungary won the support of the disparate Turkish empire and Bulgaria. Meanwhile, Japan, America and Italy lined up on the side of Britain and her allies.

It would, they said in Britain, all be over by Christmas. In fact, it rumbled on for four bloody years, as both sides sacrificed thousands of lives daily for a few feet of territory. In effect, those two shots in Sarajevo killed no less than ten million men.

Grigori Rasputin

To his enemies he was an evil crank. Vulgar and filthy, the menacing monk Rasputin was loathed and despised by many of the Russian aristocracy.

Yet to others, he was a saint whose penetrating eyes were beacons of hope and whose coarse outpourings were, in fact, wise prophecies. No matter that his beard was matted, his fingernails grimy and his sexual appetite boundless. His supporters believed that only he was capable of steering a troubled Russia to a bright new future.

From humble beginnings, Rasputin successfully charmed his way into Russian society, finding favour with Alexandra Feodorovna, wife of the autocratic ruler, Tsar Nicholas II. Thanks to the healing powers he appeared to exert on their sickly son Alexis, the monk was given unprecedented power in the Tsar's court. When Nicholas went off to the front to see for himself the ravages of World War I, it seemed to many that this grubby peasant had the country in the palm of his hand.

It was too much to bear for one Russian prince who recruited a handful of friends to help free his beloved country from the curse of the mad monk once and for all - by killing him. As they plotted, they could not have known what a difficult task they had chosen.

Rasputin was born Grigori Efimovich in Siberia in 1871, the son of a drunken thief and a child bride. In his youth, he earned the title of Rasputin, meaning debauched woman-chaser, due to his frolics with village girls. Despite having a wife and three children, he continued with this lecherous behaviour until he received a sudden calling for religion. He joined the Khlisty sect, or Flagellants, as they

Rasputin surrounded by Empress Alexandra and her children.

were otherwise known, famous for their sexual licence.

Perhaps it was his piercing eyes which earned him fame initially. Maybe it was the electrifying rhetoric which he delivered with gusto or his apparent gift for curing all manner of ills. Whatever the reason, women fell at his feet in droves. He preached that sex would be their salvation and found plenty of women, old and young, rich and poor, willing to subscribe to his ideas. It is said that he even raped a nun.

Soon he arrived in the capital, St. Petersburg, where word of the charismatic Rasputin reached the royal ears. As he swaggered in for his first audience with the lofty Tsar and Tsarina in 1908, Rasputin looked more monster than miracle-worker. Yet he stemmed the flow of blood from the gaping wounds the 4-year-old Tsarevich sustained even from the smallest knock. The Tsarevich, Alexis, suffered from haemophilia, a condition inherited from his mother, which meant that his blood did not clot and cuts and bruises would not heal easily.

Whether by hypnosis or by a genuine ability to heal, Rasputin appeared to be the answer to the prayers of the anxious parents. Under his care, Alexis grew stronger and looked healthier. The Tsarina was convinced of his powers and wanted him to stay close by in case of relapses.

It gave Rasputin a unique place in society. He gathered around him an entourage of women who would gladly do his bidding - in bed and around the house - convinced that he was a prophet. He gained a particular thrill in recruiting the wives of important ministers or officers into his cosy band, giving him an ever-widening power base.

Soon he was in a position to nominate people for plum jobs in the church and government. Those who curried favour with him (and paid him cash) would be recruited for the top jobs. Anyone who was even mildly opposed to him and his dubious methods were laughed out of court. His enemies were banished to the snowy wastes of Siberia from whence he had come.

His persuasive personal magnetism won him many admirers. With the protection of the Tsarina, Rasputin's depraved lifestyle continued unchecked. But he also made many enemies who believed he was nothing more than a charlatan. He became a prime target for assassination.

A disgruntled prostitute, Khinia Gureva, tried to kill him in 1914 when he visited his native village. Even though she plunged a dagger into his stomach up to the hilt, Rasputin lived. His attacker was later sent to an asylum. The Tsarina was appalled by the incident, believing her son's only hope of survival had almost been snatched from him. So this attack merely strengthened his position in the capital.

Rasputin's incredible physical strength in the face of such a fierce assault should have given fair warning to the men who decided to murder him two years later. The leader was Prince Felix Yusopov, from one of the oldest and richest families in the country. His cohorts were Grand Duke Dmitri Pavlovich, cousin to the Tsar, politician Vladimir Purishkevich, army doctor Lazovert and Captain Sergei Soukhotin, veteran of the front line fighting. They were not only fearful of the influence which Rasputin exerted at court, but also certain that the monk, notorious for his opposition to Russia's involvement in World War I, was seeking a negotiated peace with Germany.

A plan was made to lure Rasputin to the Moika Palace, lavish home of the Yusopovs, with a faked invitation from the lovely Princess Irina, wife of Prince Felix. There they would poison him with cyanide and then dump his dead body in the river.

The plan progressed well when Rasputin readily accepted the invitation, timed for midnight on 29th December, 1916. The monk was eager to seduce the attractive princess who would be a valuable asset to his 'harem' of women.

Yusupov accompanied his victim to a basement room in the richly appointed palace, claiming that Princess Irina had been delayed. He watched as Rasputin ate one cake injected with enough poison to kill a man, then another. Both were washed down with generous quantities of wine laced with deadly cyanide. Yet there seemed to be no ill effects in the lanky, lean figure of the monk. Rather he appeared more lively than ever, seeking music and song for entertainment. Yusopov was astounded and alarmed. Was the man indestructible? He made an excuse and escaped to consult with the other conspirators. They agreed that they would have to shoot Rasputin.

Back downstairs, Yusupov asked his prey to examine a crucifix. A moment later he produced a pistol and blasted it off at Rasputin at point-blank range. The monk collapsed on the floor, apparently dead.

Yusupov joined the others who were making preparations for removing the corpse from the palace. He returned to the room where the lifeless body lay and checked once again to ensure there was no pulse. To his horror, one of Rasputin's eyes twitched open, then the other. The next minute Rasputin was grappling with the frightened Prince, still strong enough to rip his uniform despite the dose of poison and the bullet still inside him.

Yusupov wrenched himself free and sped off to find his gun again. Rasputin followed him out and was rampaging around the palace courtyard roaring threats to Yusupov:

'Felix, I will tell the Tsarina,' he pledged.

By now Purishkevich had appeared with his revolver and fired four shots at the demented monk. Two found their target and Rasputin once again lay prone on the floor. Yusupov was taking no chances this time. He grabbed an iron bar and beat the body until it was virtually unrecognisable. The intense drama had clearly shocked him. He was later to regret the loss of control which led to such a brutal act on a critically injured man.

The shots had attracted the interest of a local policeman. He was dispatched with a bribe. The gang wrapped the body in canvas and drove to a bridge where they pitched it into the fast-flowing, icy waters.

It was three days before Rasputin was found. A postmortem revealed he had water in his lungs. That meant he was almost certainly alive when he entered the water. Russia's Tsarina was inconsolable. She arranged an extravagant funeral for the man she adored.

Anxious members of the middle and upper classes were delighted that the scourge of the monarchy was gone forever. Crucially, however, a significant number of peasants who viewed him as a hero saw it as yet another example of the gentry crushing their hopes and opportunities.

His body lay in peace for only a few months. Revolution had come to Russia and before long vengeful soldiers exhumed Rasputin's coffin, believing it to be a symbol of the corrupt Royal regime, and burnt his body in a woodland clearing. His ashes were scattered in the snow.

As for the Tsarina, her desire for revenge against the perpetrators of the killing was short-lived. The dynasty which her husband led was toppled and, after months in jail, she was killed alongside the rest of her family, including her beloved Alexis.

Tsar Nicholas II

By the time Tsar Nicholas II came to the throne in 1894, Russia was already on the way to revolution. An introverted, handsome, but seemingly easily-led prince, it was his misfortune that he was not very bright and was totally incapable of ruling a country as vast and complex as the one he inherited. Many of the reforms his grandfather had instituted had been overturned by his father and, faced with increasing social unrest, he was indecisive and unable to face up to reality.

His young wife, Alexandra Feodorovna, further sowed the seeds of discontent by seeming aloof and distanced from the people. In May 1898, while taking part in a ceremony that ended with the dispensing of gifts to the masses, she left early to go to a ball. The people, believing the gifts were running out, rioted and hundreds died in the crush.

She and her husband were doubtless unaware of the tragedy as they danced the night away. But the damage had been done and the Romanovs were perceived as being increasingly remote. She was to make an even graver mistake six years later, a blunder that was carried out with the best of intentions, but which probably sealed the fate of the last Russian Tsar.

In 1904 she presented the Tsar with a male heir, Alexis. Sadly the boy suffered from the curse of the Romanovs — he was a haemophiliac and not expected to live beyond the age of 18. In desperation, she called on the monk Rasputin. And when she saw he had some degree of healing power, she embraced his strange brand of mysticism with all the fervour of a religious bigot. Worse, she was able to per-

Tsar Nicholas II and his family: Empress Alexandra,
son Alexis and three of his four daughters – Olga,
Tatania and Marie.

suade the Tsar to follow the mad monk's teachings. Rasputin's influence at court was starting to grow.

Not surprisingly, the Russian nobility and bourgeoisie resented the power of the upstart peasant monk, but, at the same time, their security was under threat from something even more sinister and inexorable - fuelled by poverty and hunger, the revolutionary movement was gaining strength. The Social Democratic Labour Party was founded in 1898. By 1901 there was a thriving Socialist Revolutionary Party. Calls for constitutional government increased.

As ever, Tsar Nicholas was indecisive. Whenever a crisis arose, he took his family to their country palace at Tsarskoe Selo, fifteen miles from St. Petersburg. All he achieved was to increase the alienation and isolation of the Romanovs. When he went to war with Japan in 1904 - an adventure that was memorable for its bungling and corruption and ended in humiliation - the revolutionary underground erupted onto the streets.

In January 1905, a group of metalworkers marched to the Winter Palace. Their intent was peaceful and their leader, the priest Georgi Gapon, wrote to the Tsar asking him to receive a petition and address the crowd. Nicholas followed his usual procedure and fled with his family to Selo.

Meanwhile, the soldiers left to guard the palace panicked when they saw the crowd and fired volley after volley into the defenceless ranks of men, women and children, killing five hundred and injuring thousands more. It was the beginning of the 1905 revolution. By the end of the year, one thousand five hundred government officials were dead.

Riots, assassinations and several naval mutinies rocked the country. In October there was a general strike. A measure of peace was restored only when the Tsar was persuaded to sign a manifesto promising reforms and the setting up of the Duma, a kind of parliament. Even then, Nicholas dissolved it several times, only to be forced to reopen it along reformed lines.

The situation was calmed only by the outbreak of World War I, when patriotic fervour united sworn enemies. However, when the Tsar took personal command of his armies, he left the government in the hands of the Tsarina - or rather in the hands of Rasputin. Now not only the militants among the masses, but also the enraged members of the nobility were plotting the downfall of the Romanovs.

Rasputin was their first victim in 1916. He was butchered, not by the proletariat, but by aristocrats. The government was paralysed by unrest.

Nicholas returned home in 1917 but the situation still deteriorated. Severe winter conditions caused food shortages. Bread was rationed and malcontents roamed the streets. At the same time, Lenin returned from exile, preaching violent revolution.

On 8th March, Nicholas again sought refuge in Selo - and the Russian Revolution started in earnest.

For a week, violent demonstrations raged across the country. Strikes became riots, police stations and law courts were looted and burned and the army mutinied. On 15th March, Nicholas accepted the inevitable end of the Romanov dynasty and abdicated in favour of the Grand Duke Michael Alexandrovitch.

The royal family was placed in protective custody in the Selo Palace they loved so much. There they remained until 14th August, when talk of a raid on the palace to liberate them forced the provisional government to remove them to Tobolsk, in Siberia. Meanwhile, the Bolsheviks under Lenin and Trotsky had assumed control. So in April, 1918 the Romanovs were again uprooted and moved to Ekaterinburg (now called Sverdlovsk) in the Ural Mountains, near Czechoslovakia. Here they were in the hands of a revolutionary Soviet and were imprisoned in a merchant's house under the strictest security.

Their guards were peasant soldiers who were not unfriendly. However, on 4th July they were replaced by secret police under the command of Jakov Jurovsky. These were not guards ... they were executioners.

In Moscow, the Bolshevik seat of government, Trotsky was trying to organise a show trial of the Tsar. He was opposed by Lenin, who feared Nicholas might conduct himself with sufficient dignity to win some support from the people. He was also violently opposed by the leader of the Ural Soviet, Isiah Goloshchekin, who wanted to kill the whole hated family.

On 12th July their fate was placed in the hands of the Ural Soviet. The next day, as the White Army, reinforced by Czech anti-Bolshevik units, beat back the ill-equipped Red Army and closed in on Ekaterinburg, the order was issued to kill the entire royal family.

Yurovsky chose a derelict mineshaft for the disposal of the bodies. Other members of the Ural Soviet bought drums of petrol and sulphuric acid. On 16th July, Yurovsky dismissed all the guards except his own secret policemen. At 7pm he ordered twelve revolvers for himself and his men.

At midnight, he woke the Tsar and told him that anti-revolutionary forces were approaching the town and they were to be moved. The family and their servants were taken to a cellar. There, they were told, they were to await transport to a safer place.

TSAR
NICHOLAS
II

Bones of a Tsar: the recently unearthed remains of Tsar Nicholas II.

What took place in that dingy cellar, with a heavy iron grill barring its only window, is still not known for certain.

The assumed scenario is that Yurovsky and his men entered and informed the group of family and servants that they were to be shot. As the Tsar rose to protest, Yurovsky fired a bullet into his head. A fusillade cut down the Tsarina and three of her daughters, along with two servants and the family doctor.

More soldiers entered carrying rifles with fixed bayonets and accounted for any other adults still standing. The family's pet dog had its skull smashed in by a rifle butt. The Tsar's son, Alexis, had been wounded, and when he stirred .was stamped to death by soldiers. Yurovsky administered the coup de grace, placing his pistol to the boy's ear and firing two shots.

The bodies were bundled into lorries and driven along the lonely route to a mineshaft, where they were mutilated and buried. They did not remain there long, however, because word quickly spread of their whereabouts, and the White Army was closing in. A day or so later, they were removed to a secret resting place deep in the forest.

The wholesale massacre of the Russian royal family was both a severance of all links with an imperial past and an exercise in terror. Trotsky himself said the murders were necessary to dishearten anti-revolutionary forces and to persuade Bolsheviks that they had passed the point of no return. It was victory or death from that point on. They were all accomplices now.

The unleashing of official State terror had the desired effect - and no-one learned the lesson better than the young Josef Stalin. It is the supreme irony that, just a few years later, Stalin would apply the terror tactics of that night in Ekaterinburg to the people of the Soviet Union, having first brought about the death of his principal rival for power, Leon Trotsky.

According to legend, one of the Tsar's daughters, Anastasia, escaped the carnage. Over the years, a number of women have claimed to be the princess and hence the heir to the Romanov fortune. Official Soviet records show that Anastasia was killed on that fatal night in 1918, and that no-one escaped.

What is certain is that a collection of bones discovered by accident in 1991 in the forest near Sverdlovsk are those of the Romanov family. That much has been proved by DNA testing, assisted by Britain's Duke of Edinburgh, who is related to the Russian royal family. However, the tests could not distinguish between the sisters.

Pancho Villa

As the flaming sun sank low in the sky, a stallion and its fugitive rider disappeared into the dim and shadowy hills. The clouds of dust kicked up by the horse's thudding hooves slowly mingling with the trailing heat haze were the only traces left behind. By the time lawmen were on the trail, it had gone cold. Pancho Villa lived to fight another day.

For many he was a Hollywood style hero in the flesh, a romantic Robin Hood who robbed the rich and divided his spoils among the poor of his native Mexico. When he rode off into the sunset, hundreds sighed in admiration.

Of course, in hard focus, he was a barbarous killer and thief who took no prisoners - he preferred to kill them. He held sway in northern Mexico at a time when savagery and slaughter were the norm.

Villa was born Doroteo Arango in 1878 in a small mining community in the state of Durango. He trained in butchery, although the blood on his hands then was but a tiny fraction of the amount that would stain them in the years to come. Like other fiery young men, he was no doubt sickened by the poverty of his neighbours and bored with the slog of work. Yet when he took to the hills as a bandit, it was with true dramatic flourish.

It happened after he discovered that one of the owners of an estate in the region had raped his sister. He killed the man, changed his name and vanished before the law could catch up with him.

At first, he was a work-a-day outlaw, rustling cattle and raiding mining headquarters. He was accompanied by a loyal band of brigands who happily carried out his bid-

Hero of the people, Pancho Villa, in full flight.

ding. Villa earned a special place in the heart of local people by leaving them generous amounts of his booty.

This shred of social conscience escalated as the years went by and was sufficient to have him join forces in revolution with the liberal Francisco Madero.

Unlike Villa, Madero came from a wealthy background. Yet despite his privileged upbringing, he was opposed to dictator President Porfirio Diaz, who for thirty-five years had kept the majority of the population in chains of poverty.

Madero initiated the Mexican revolution of 1910 with the help of Villa, who put his highly-trained army of men at Madero's disposal. For his efforts, Villa was made a colonel and, with his new-found respectability, strove to become a businessman. His new honest Pancho persona was not to last long.

The newly-installed President Madero was dismissed as weak by his enemies on both the left and the right. Even US ambassador, Henry Lane Wilson, was disenchanted with him. He was the subject of numerous assassination plots, many brewed in the ranks of his own armed forces. Villa was soon back in action fighting for the survival of the revolution.

So treacherous were the Mexican generals of the time, that Villa found himself accused of insubordination by a former comrade and was condemned to death by firing squad. In true storybook fashion, he was standing with his back against an adobe wall and a line of troops were taking aim when President Madero's brother Raul appeared waving a reprieve.

In the belief that the politics of Mexico were too hot to handle, Villa fled to America in 1912. While he was away, the man who signed his death warrant, General Victoriano

Huerta, overthrew Madero and ordered that his predecessor be killed. Madero was cold-bloodedly shot in the back of the head by an army major who later told the world that he fired when the well-meaning ex-president had tried to escape.

Villa returned to arms to rout the new dictator along with other supporters of the 1910 revolution. In 1914 Villa won the day. Huerta resigned and one of Villa's colleagues, General Emillio Carranza, became president.

It should have meant peace, at least for a while. But Villa was soon unhappy at the direction taken by Carranza. His concern remained chiefly for his poor and unrepresented countrymen. So he joined forces with another insurgent, Emiliano Zapata, and briefly occupied the capital, Mexico City. This time he did not achieve the fairy-tale ending that so frequently accompanied his escapades. He was beaten back to the territories in the north where he was best loved. He lay low there for a while, seething at the conservatism of the Carranza regime.

Hemmed in by Carranza's men in the south, Villa was forced to look towards America as a source of supplies. He crossed the border and blasted his way through Columbus, New Mexico, leaving nine civilians and eight soldiers fatally wounded.

US President Woodrow Wilson was outraged. He dispatched a division of men under the command of General 'Black Jack' Pershing to bring back Villa, dead or alive. Pershing was determined to get his man. But he reckoned without the loyalty of local peasants to Villa and the inefficiency of the Mexican government. Information about the elusive Villa was hard to come by and he lost valuable time tracking leads that led nowhere. Nine months after first entering Mexico, Pershing and his men had their one and only chance to trap Villa.

The bandit was ambushed. There was a pitched battle between Americans and Mexicans in which Villa was shot in the leg three times. Although gravely ill, he was whisked from the conflict to a mountain cave where it took weeks to recover his health. Pershing gave up the chase. It had cost the US government $130 million and had all been in vain.

It did persuade Villa, however, that it was time to retire. Even the joys of thinking up new and macabre ways for his prisoners and enemies to die were beginning to pale. In July 1920 he and nine hundred of his men gave themselves up to the government, now led by Adolfo de la Huerta. Villa was rewarded for his actions by the gift of a 25,000 acre ranch in his home province of Durango, as well as thousands of dollars. At last, Villa had the cash to put his ideas into action. He built a hospital, chapel, school and telegraph office in the town of Parral where he became a familiar figure, flanked by an army of bodyguards.

The political giants of the day were still uneasy, believing that Villa could once again spark blood-letting for his own ends. Indeed, he did side with Adolfo de la Huerta who was to be a major player in the elections proposed for 1924. No-one can tell what Villa's actions might have been. For on 20th July, 1923 he was cut down in a hail of bullets as the early morning sunshine beat down on Parral.

Villa was in his distinctive Ford Dodge along with his right-hand man, Colonel Miguel Trillo, going into town for supplies. More than a hundred bullets were fired by the assassins who were lining both sides of the street. Nine bullets pierced his body. Trillo, five bodyguards, the chauffeur and a civilian were also killed.

What of the man who snuffed out the life of a legend? The leader of the assassination conspirators was a little-known congressman, Jesus Salas Barrazas, who was determined not just to wipe Villa from the face of politics but also to avenge a massacre by the bandit years before. Barrazas claimed he wanted the reward due from the US government to go to families of Villa's many victims. He was jailed for twenty years, but quickly released when it became clear he was in mortal danger behind bars from vengeful Villa supporters. In fact, all but one of the assassins met a violent end. One was even cut down at the same spot as Villa.

Now accorded the status of hero in Mexico, Villa, who lived and died by the gun, is mostly remembered for the progress which he made in his campaigns on behalf of the poor and meek. Historian, Samuel H. Mayo, sums him up in rather a different light: 'He could be warm and friendly at one moment and ferocious the next. He could invite you to dinner and then order your execution, rescind the order and offer you coffee.'

Huey Long

He started life as a humble farm boy from Winnfield, Louisiana, but anyone who knew Huey Long realised he was destined for greater things. From the moment he began work as a salesman, through his rise as a brilliant young lawyer and finally into politics, Long was a special breed. He knew what he wanted and usually he got it.

In 1928, when he was just 35, he reached the first milestone on what he hoped would be the road to the White House. Voters endorsed him in their thousands as Louisiana state governor and he immediately set about implementing the massive programme of social reforms with which he had wooed the people. As well as cultivating his image as friend of the working family, Long devoted his early term to badly needed infrastructure projects such as roads and bridge-building, more state-run hospitals and more schools for poverty-stricken rural areas. To the casual observer he was champion of the poor, the underprivileged, the sick and the old.

Good intentions were one thing. The methods by which the masterplan was being put into action was quite another. Huey Long quickly became frustrated by the delays and (as he saw it) red tape of the democratic process. He regarded himself as a mover and fixer and believed that the end always justified the means. He saw nothing wrong with patronage to help lever his proposals through the legislature and looked to 'imaginative' sources to help fund his political ambitions.

Such sources included the Mafia. When New York City Mayor Fiorello H. LaGuardia hounded the Mob's slot machine empire out of the Big Apple, Long instantly saw dollar signs popping up before his eyes. He invited Godfather Frank Costello to discuss with him a plan for moving the entire operation into New Orleans. A deal was struck, the Mafia was back in business and Long's political fighting fund got the expected healthy boost.

Throughout those first years as state governor, Long seemed to relish controversy. On one occasion in 1929 he called a special sitting of the legislature to ram through a punitive new tax on the oil business. Emotions ran high throughout the debate with punches being traded openly on the floor of the state's House of Representatives. Hours later the House not only scuppered Long's bill but voted to impeach him on charges of bribery and misconduct. He was never convicted.

Then there was the fiasco surrounding his election to the US Senate. Long won his seat in 1930 but refused to take it up for eighteen months amid fears that Louisiana's Lieutenant Governor, Paul N. Cyr, would take over the governorship of Louisiana and dismantle the power base he had so carefully constructed. Twice during this period, Cyr got himself sworn in - but, in a remarkable display of brinkmanship, Long managed to turn out the National Guard just as the succession was due to take effect. Such was the troopers' loyalty, that they unhesitatingly surrounded the executive mansion and the highway commission to prevent the Cyr camp from moving in.

To outsiders, the Long school of politics had some nasty parallels in Europe. Had not a charismatic leader called Adolf Hitler taken an iron grip on Germany by harnessing the workers' support and then dismantling democracy? And in Italy hadn't Mussolini won popularity initially by building better roads and improving the reliability of the railway network?

If Long heard the critics, he ignored them. By 1934 he had conjured up an outrageous political reform which effectively installed him as dictator for the state of Louisiana. He made it a crime punishable by jail for Federal officials to promote Franklin D. Roosevelt's New Deal for the poor within Louisiana state boundaries. Long had once been a supporter of Roosevelt; now he saw him as a barrier to his own presidential ambitions. Long had his own social reforms - he didn't want the people to be seduced by his rival's.

Such was the gerrymandering, that electoral boundaries were re-designed to ensure that Long's supporters retained their seats, while opponents were booted out. One of those opponents was the vociferous Judge Pavy of Opelousas, a critic of the Long administration. The judge's son-in-law was mild-mannered physician, Dr. Carl Weiss, a respected ear, eye, nose and throat specialist.

To this day it is unclear why Dr. Weiss, aged 29, decided to kill Huey Long. Was it out of personal loyalty to the judge? A sense that democracy needed a hand to survive a tyrant's rule? Or was it down to jealousy - the suggestion that Long had begun a relationship with Weiss's wife?

All three motives loomed large in the best-selling thriller by Robert Penn Warren, *All the King's Men*. Although supposedly a work of fiction, the events in the novel bear a striking similarity to the rise and fall of 'The Kingfish' (Long's nickname in Louisiana). To this day fact and fiction have become merged to the extent that no-one really knows the truth behind the assassination.

What is known is that, on the night of 8th September, 1935, Weiss, dressed in a distinctive white linen suit, kissed his wife goodbye, claiming that he needed to make a round of house calls. Instead he drove directly to the Baton Rouge Capitol Building and loitered in the corridor near the office of Oscar Allen, one of Long's closest political allies. Later some witnesses would tell how the doctor murmured 'it won't be long now' as he strode nervously around the hallway.

Just before 9.30 pm the legislature broke up and Long, accompanied by Supreme Court Justice John Fournet and a ring of bodyguards, stormed out of the chamber in his usual businesslike fashion. Typically, he was shouting orders at his minions as he went: 'Everybody be here in the morning. Tell everybody to be here.' As he spoke, no-one registered the fact that Carl Weiss had stepped quietly from the side of the corridor to stroll a few steps at Long's side.

Seconds later Weiss drew his Belgian-made .32 calibre pistol, rammed it into the senator's side and squeezed off a round. Long staggered back in pain and shock as Justice Fournet and bodyguard Murphy Roden went for Weiss's arm.

There was a brief wrestling match, then Long's body-guards levelled their sub-machine guns to offload a lethal shower of lead into the killer. Weiss's body was jumping around a full minute after he was dead as the troopers continued to pump bullets into him. The post-mortem examination later showed that he had been struck by thirty rounds in the chest, twenty-nine in the back and two in the head.

As the gunfire cracked, Huey Long staggered down a stairway in the Capitol Building and collapsed into the arms of his Public Service Commissioner, James O' Connor. 'Jimmy, my boy, I'm shot,' were the only words he could manage, a trickle of blood running from the corner of his mouth.

O'Connor, believing that he was up against a small army of assassins judging by the gunshots nearby, drew his own revolver and dragged his boss to a taxi outside. Minutes later Long was in a hospital operating theatre as doctors prepared to administer a massive blood transfusion in readiness for emergency surgery. There was no time for an anaesthetist and Long didn't care: 'Go ahead and clean the wound,' he ordered.

It was no use. At 4.10 pm, after two blood transfusions, Huey Long died from bullet wounds to his stomach and kidney.

Within days the rumour-mill was turning out the so-called 'truth' about the way the Senator died. There was one claim that Weiss never managed to fire a shot but was gunned down by Long's bodyguards. In the heat of the moment these guards, it was alleged, also shot the man they were paid to protect. A third version of events has it that Weiss never wanted to kill his target, only humiliate him in public by punching him on the jaw. Neither of these accounts seems to be supported by the facts.

For all his abilities as a wheeler-dealer, Long accumulated comparatively little wealth in his short life. There was no will, a few shares in oil companies of questionable worth, a New Orleans home that was heavily mortgaged and about $130,000 worth of life insurance. Commentators argued that almost the whole of his hidden fortune had gone towards promoting his political image, funding his newspaer *The American Progress* and laying the groundwork for his Presidential campaign.

The true reasons for the assassination will never be known. Certainly Carl Weiss shared his plans with nobody, and, although a Senate inquiry was later convened, there was never an iota of evidence to suggest that the doctor was part of some wider, more sinister conspiracy. The most likely explanation is that Weiss had a personal grudge and a death wish. No politician can guard against men like him.

Carl Weiss's funeral was held two days after the killing of Huey Long. Whatever else he may have been, he died a popular man. More than a thousand mourners attended the service, including some senior politicians. Long's state funeral that same week attracted a crowd of thirty thousand.

Leon Trotsky

In 1940 there were two giants of Communism vying for world attention. Together, Leon Trotsky and Joseph Stalin would have been an awesome force - yet they loathed and detested one another. The world was not big enough to contain these vicious sparring partners and Stalin ensured that it was he who survived.

Both Trotsky and Stalin pulled together under the leadership of Lenin to overthrow the royal rulers of imperial Russia in 1917. However, on the death of Lenin, the father of the revolution, their petty squabble erupted into a raging feud of harsh words and poisonous politics.

Soon in exile, Trotsky reserved his most vitriolic and scathing criticisms for Stalin, then ruler of communist Russia. In reply, Stalin had his bitter enemy killed.

The roots of their mutual hatred ran as deep as the reasons for the Russian revolt itself. They shared a humble background and early conversion to Marxism, which first appeared as a significant force during the 1890s. Both were keenly ambitious and each was as objectionable as the other. They were, by all accounts, cold-hearted, ruthless and determined.

Trotsky, it seemed, was the natural successor to Lenin, having been his second-in-command. Stalin badly wanted the top job and was prepared to go to any lengths to get it. He didn't have long to wait before seizing his opportunity.

When it came to the future of Communism, their opinions differed significantly. Stalin wanted to consolidate the strength of the new-found communist state in Russia. Trotsky yearned to take the revolution world-wide. It was Stalin's stance that found most favour with the leading

Trotsky (front row, second from right) with his 'allies' and fellow
revolutionaries, Stalin (marked by XX) and Kruschev (marked by X).

The ice axe that Frank Jackson used to kill Trotsky.

lights of the Communist party in Russia and he used this as a lever to oust Trotsky just a few years after Lenin died.

Trotsky was born Lev Bronstein, son of Jewish parents in the Ukraine, in 1879. Before he reached his 20th birthday he had already been arrested as a revolutionary. After three months of solitary confinement he was transported to the snowy outpost of Siberia. From there he escaped and joined his fellow Marxist, Vladimir Illyich Lenin, in London in 1902.

The Tsarist regime in Russia was almost overthrown in 1905. Tsar Nicholas II once again affirmed that he would not consider a democracy. In addition, his troops opened fire on protesting peasants who were peaceably demonstrating against poor pay and conditions. A wave of civil disruption followed, including strikes and assassinations. The armed forces were poised to mutiny. By October, the Tsar promised to establish a parliament, the 'Duma', and a prime minister was appointed. It was enough to satisfy the majority of the protestors.

Hardline revolutionaries like Trotsky and Lenin had dashed back to their homeland in the hope of fermenting enough trouble to topple the Imperialist system. Instead, the coup fizzled out.

Trotsky was arrested and returned to Siberia once more. Again he escaped, travelling between refuges set up by like-minded socialists across Europe until 1917, when revolution reared again in Russia.

This time there was no stopping it. The people were fed up with fighting in World War I, which had claimed millions of lives and caused appalling hardship. Unrest swept through the country, the royal family was taken prisoner and opulent houses belonging to the nobility were taken over by hordes of insurgents.

Inevitably, there was a backlash from the upper ranks of the army who could foresee their heritage and personal fortunes evaporating. Trotsky was made Commissar for War in the ensuing civil conflict. Perhaps his greatest achievement was to build the Red Army from a ragged bunch of just ten thousand men into a mammoth force numbering five million. With the fine fighting men he commanded, the 'Whites', who sought to reverse the revolution, were seen off. Trotsky was Russia's second most powerful man.

In the wings, however, was Stalin. Born in Georgia to a cobbler, he was expelled from religious training in 1899 for his extreme political views. He was also sent to Siberia and spent years in exile, waiting for the wind of change in his homeland.

He was influential as editor of the Communist newspaper, *Pravda*, during the revolution and won a place in Lenin's government as Commissar for Nationalities. In 1922 he became secretary of the Communist party. It wasn't enough to satisfy his lust for power. No sooner had Lenin been ceremonially interred following his death in January, 1924, than Stalin announced himself as new leader of the country.

Despite being an architect of the revolution, Trotsky was unable to counter Stalin's skilful manipulation of the party hierarchy. First he was sacked from his post as Commissar of War. Then, in 1927, he was expelled from the Communist Party which he had helped to create. Two years later he was deported.

Trotsky was granted asylum in Turkey. From there he moved to France, then Norway, which he was forced to leave in 1936. He then made his home in Mexico, aware that his enemy, Stalin, was baying for his blood.

Stalin was no match for the biting intellect of Trotsky and he knew it. His rule held fast through politics of terror rather than intelligent diplomacy or reasoned argument. He became an easy target for Trotsky, who chose not the sword but the pen to wound. He produced pieces entitled 'The Stalinist School of Falsification', 'Stalin's Crimes' and 'The Real Situation in Russia'. He also planned a derogatory autobiography of the leader.

Writer George Bernard Shaw summed up Trotsky's talents: 'When he cuts off his opponent's head, he holds it up to show that there are no brains in it.'

While Stalin tightened his grip on Russia during the 1930s, Trotsky stepped up his literary assassinations. He risked all by incurring the wrath of the moustachioed dictator who detested criticism even in its mildest form. In 1938, there came the first indication of what lay ahead. Trotsky's 32-year-old son, Lev Sedov, was snatched from his hospital bed in Paris and murdered by Stalinist agents. Then came the first attack against Trotsky himself.

Painter and Stalinist, David Alfaro Siqueiros, led a twenty man assault on Trotsky's home in Mexico City. As they burst into the bedroom, the attackers, wearing fake police uniforms, sprayed an estimated three hundred rounds of ammunition into the walls. By a miracle, Trotsky and his wife survived by lying flat on the floor.

Siqueiros and his bandits fled, taking with them a 23-year-old American who was employed as a guard by Trotsky. The body of wealthy rebel, Sheldon Harte, was found weeks later riddled with gunfire in a house nearby. Mexican communists - who at first believed the incident to be a stunt staged by Trotsky himself - disowned Siqueiros as a renegade. Yet already the hired thug had quit the country to escape justice.

Trotsky was now painfully aware that his life was on the line. He transformed his home into a fortress. Machine-gun stations were installed high on 15 foot walls, a steel door protected the entrance and an army of guards patrolled the grounds. It was clear to the Stalin camp that another violent attack would probably also fail. A more devious plot was hatched.

Stalinist agent, Ramon Mercador, was the lynchpin of the operation. Posing as an American called Frank Jackson, he seduced Sylvia Agelof, a New Yorker who enjoyed open access to Trotsky. She willingly introduced him to her mentor, believing that he would be an asset to their group, 'The Fourth International', which aimed to establish world-wide socialism. Jackson ingratiated himself with Trotsky over a number of months, becoming a regular visitor at his home for dinner and debates, and wrote numerous articles on international socialism. He spent his spare time mountain climbing.

On 20th August, 1940 Jackson arrived clutching his raincoat. The guards allowed him past without a second glance. How could they know that tucked inside the raincoat pocket was a deadly ice axe? Asking Trotsky to vet a piece he had penned, he lured the great theorist and thinker into a study where Natalia Trotsky sat quietly reading. At his request, she rose to get Jackson a glass of water.

Behind closed doors, the voices were raised sharply - until a sudden, blood-curdling scream rang out. Guards and Mrs Trotsky burst into the room to find a shocking scene.

Mercador himself later described the events: 'I took the piolet (ice axe) out of my raincoat, took it in my fist and, closing my eyes, I gave him a tremendous blow on the head. The man screamed in such a way that I will never forget as long as I live. His scream was very long, infinitely long, and it still seems to me as if that scream were piercing my brains.'

He tried to deliver a second blow but, despite his terrible injury, Trotsky grabbed his hand and bit it. Guards pounced on Mercador and gave him a violent beating. Trotsky was asked if his attacker should be killed. Racked with pain, he answered: 'Impermissible to kill. He must be forced to talk.'

Both injured men were rushed to the same hospital. While Mercador made a good recovery, Trotsky died twenty-six hours later from the devastating injuries to his brain. Before he died, he uttered: 'Stalin has finally accomplished the task he unsuccessfully attempted before.'

Trotsky never knew that Mercador was in fact the son of Stalin agent and dedicated Cuba-based communist Caridad, who was sitting outside when the attack took place. She had convinced her son that the traitor Trotsky had to die for the sake of the revolution and the good of communism. Just around the corner to the Trotsky home was Kremlin chief, Leonid Eitingon, otherwise known as General Kotov. Although he never admitted it, all the indications were that Mercador was working on Stalin's orders.

United States officials blocked attempts to take Trotsky's body there for burial. He was cremated in Mexico City six days after his death.

It was months before Mercador came to trial. Syvlia Agelof was also arrested but was freed when all charges against her were dropped. Finally, in 1943, the assassin was sentenced to twenty years behind bars. He served seventeen years before being released and leaving Mexico to start a new life in Czechoslovakia. Like his mother before him, he was declared a national hero in the Soviet Union. He died in Havana in 1978 ... still haunted by the screams of his victim.

Mahatma Gandhi

It somehow seems more fitting for men of violence to die by the bomb or the bullet than to see a man of peace cut down in an ugly fit of aggression.

When Mahatma Gandhi was killed by the gun of an assassin, even his enemies and rivals suffered pangs of sorrow. Gandhi, the liberator of India, had proved beyond all doubt that peace was every bit as effective as arms when it came to winning battles. Yet the frail guru was slain in a burst of violence by someone who could find no better answer to the politics of peace.

This spiritual leader of the subcontinent - and conscience of the world - was born Mohandas Gandhi in Western India on 2nd October, 1869. By 1888 he had left for England to study law, which he put to good use in his home country for several years before moving to South Africa. There, he started campaigning for his fellow Indians, who were treated as second-class citizens. To achieve his ends, he resorted to passive protests with considerable success.

He returned to India in 1914, determined to bring British colonial rule there to an end. Even before his sandal-clad feet trod Indian soil again, he was heralded as a saviour by many Indians. So respected was he, that he was quickly elected leader of the Indian National Congress, the political party launched in 1885 which sought home rule. Gandhi encouraged his growing band of followers to pursue a policy of 'satyagraha', a Sanskrit expression for non-violent resistance. It also extended to civil disobedience, such as the non-payment of British taxes.

The British, meanwhile, were full of trepidation about

Mahatma Gandhi: the man of peace meanders along a Bombay seashore.

the slight figure who was the undisputed spiritual leader of this prized colony. He disconcerted them by his peaceful perseverance. Atrocities committed against the Indians by the British did little to dent his morale or his fortitude. In frustration, they jailed him in 1922 with a hefty six year sentence. After two years, he was freed 'for health reasons'.

On his release, he stepped back from Indian politics to tour his homeland. His concern was for the 'untouchables', those unfortunates on the bottom rung of the Hindu caste system thought to defile members of higher orders with merely the brush of a hand.

The devout Gandhi was appalled by the suffering and misery of the untouchables and endeavoured to make Indians rethink their attitudes. His personal efforts and deprivations during this time won him admiration from many who thought him a saint. In recognition, he was awarded the title Mahatma, or 'Great Soul'.

As if the two goals of freedom for India and the dismantling of the caste system were not enough, Gandhi also campaigned to regenerate cottage industries such as weaving and other crafts. When he returned to the arena of politics in 1927, the government monopoly on salt production was the object of his passion. By way of protest, he led a walk from Ahmedabad to the sea, some two hundred miles, to distill some salt at the coast. His reward from the anxious authorities was a spell behind bars.

Freedom came in time for him to attend the Round Table Conference on India in London in 1931 as representative of the Indian National Congress. Against the grey, rain-lashed London streets, the man who wore nothing more substantial than a cotton wrap, in bare legs and sandals, presented a memorable figure.

In 1932 he undertook his first 'fast unto death' to force

the government into action on the issue of the untouchables, winning at least partial concessions. It was a ploy he continued to use to achieve victory during many future battles. A year later, Gandhi was once again wearying of the pressures of politics and withdrew to a religious retreat. But he could not resist a return to public life at the start of World War II. Here was a golden opportunity to oust the British once and for all. It was one he was ready to seize. Although he was undoubtedly filled with horror at the antics of Adolf Hitler, he fell far short of supporting the British.

By 1942, the Japanese were set to invade and conquer the sub-continent. The British government pledged independence at the end of hostilities if only Indians would lend support now. Gandhi was not impressed. He branded the offer 'a post-dated cheque on a failing bank' and demanded immediate British withdrawal. Instantly he was arrested, alongside other Congressmen, as a subversive.

Britain had realised, however, that it must relinquish its hold on India, once the jewel in the crown of its Empire. Gandhi was released to become a key negotiator in the talks on the new, independent India. Britain was insistent that two countries should be created - India for the Hindu population and Pakistan for the Muslims. There was a long history of clashes between the cultures and the partition was designed to end it.

Gandhi was fervently opposed to the idea. He firmly believed that all creeds could live together in harmony given the opportunity. It was his belief in this unity, construed wrongly as support for the Muslims, which led to his death.

Independence came to India on 15th August, 1947, rapidly followed by violent rioting between the Hindus and Muslims, which claimed thousands of lives. Gandhi's response was to stage another fast-unto-death which had the desired effect. He also toured the trouble spots to ensure that his message of peace got through to the people. Both sides modified their stance and reined in their militants and an uneasy truce was established by 1948.

Outsiders might have considered it a major success. Fanatical Hindus, however, brooded about the unforgiveable tolerance displayed by Gandhi towards the Muslims. A group of nine gathered to plan an assassination which would free them from this traitor, Gandhi.

At the head of it was 65-year-old Vinayak Damodar Savarkar, who had eight men in his team of killers. They hatched a passionate but impractical plot, in which no-one was clear about their role. Such was their incompetence, that they were spotted as they approached a house being used by Gandhi on 19th January, 1948 and forced to scatter. One was arrested. Later, it was claimed that he had confessed all to the police, including the names of all the conspirators. The police, it seems, did nothing with the knowledge. Did this indicate a desire to have a thorn in the side of the authorities removed once and for all?

Even if they had taken steps, it is unlikely that Gandhi would have accepted official protection. He once said 'If I am to die by the bullet of a madman, I must do so smiling. God must be in my heart and on my lips. And promise me one thing - should such a thing happen, you are not to shed one tear.'

It left the way clear for the murderers to try again. This time they elected one man, Nathuram V. Godse, to do the dirty deed. Godse, originally from Poona, was the editor of a Hindu nationalist newspaper. The appointed day of assassination was 30th January, 1948.

Gandhi had been up since 3.30 am studying paperwork and drawing up a draft constitution for Congress. When the time for evening prayers arrived, he broke off talks with the deputy prime minister, Sardar Patel, to make his way to a nearby prayer pavilion. Among the admiring crowd who jostled and shoved to be near the Mahatma, was Godse. With determination, he forged to the front of the crowd.

Godse pulled out a tiny revolver concealed in his shirt and fired four times. He was only two feet away from 78-year-old Gandhi and three bullets found their target. Two passed straight through his bony frame while the third lodged in his lung. Gandhi greeted death calmly, with a smile playing on his lips. He folded his hands in prayer, made a sign of forgiveness and uttered 'Hai Rama, Hai Rama' (Oh God, Oh God). The Father of India died within half an hour.

Godse dropped his weapon and surrendered. In custody, he drew up a ninety-two page document which denounced Gandhi as 'a curse to India, a force for evil'. His hatred for Gandhi was rooted in the fear that Muslims would rise up and overwhelm India, erasing the Hindu religion forever. Godse was put on trial with seven others. He and Narayan Dattatraya Apte, the production manager of his newspaper, were hanged in February of the following year.

Friend and foe alike paid tribute to Gandhi on his death. Britain's King George VI issued his sympathies to the people of India 'for the irreparable loss which they and mankind have suffered'. Pakistan's leader Quaid-I-Azam said 'Whatever our political differences, he was one of the greatest men ever produced by the Hindu community and a leader who commanded their universal confidence and respect'. Even the South African premier, Field Marshall Smuts, called Gandhi 'a prince among men'.

The mourned leader was taken to the banks of a sacred river and burned on a scented funeral pyre. Often Gandhi in his role as peace-maker had pronounced these words of wisdom: 'If blood be shed, let it be my blood. Cultivate the quiet courage of dying without killing. For man lives freely only by his readiness to die, if need be, at the hands of his brother - never by killing him.'

Anastasio Somoza

It ranks among the all-time memorable quotes of any American President: 'He's a son of a bitch, but he's our son of a bitch.'

It doesn't matter whether Franklin D. Roosevelt ever actually said those words (he almost certainly didn't). The phrase has long since won its place in US political mythology, to be repeated dozens of times a year by some Senator or Congressman in need of a neat cliché.

The quote Roosevelt may or may not have used referred to the Nicaraguan dictator, Anastasio Somoza, a man whose rule was shrouded in myths and half-truths. As the country's leader for more than twenty years, Somoza would often boast openly of his close and friendly links with Washington, even though the White House was regularly embarrassed by his contemptuous dismissal of democratic reforms and his ruthless suppression of opponents.

In later years that history of relations between the two countries would be held up by Sandinista revolutionaries as justification for a bloody civil war in which thousands of innocent civilians would die. America for its part, then led by Ronald Reagan, would be content to continue pumping money and weapons to the doomed right-wing option in Nicaragua - the Contras. Anastasio Somoza had a lot to answer for.

Somoza was born on 1st February, 1896 in San Marcos, the son of a coffee planter who was wealthy enough to send his boy to the local private school. The young Anastasio completed his higher education in Nicaragua and then moved on to the Pierce School of

The Nicaraguan dictator, Anastasio Somoza, ruthless-
ly suppressed opposition.

Business Administration in Philadelphia. It was here that he met his wife-to-be, Salvadora Debayle, and together they tried to launch a series of business ventures. It came to nothing and Somoza did what so many other business failures had done before him; he became a politician.

At that time US influence throughout the Americas was all-powerful. By the turn of the century American military might had seen off the Spanish stake in Cuba and started to exclude some major world powers from the Panama Canal. In 1909 a force of four hundred US marines was sent in to Nicaragua to help the rebel forces of General Juan Estrada in his attempt to overthrow the ruling President Zelaya. Zelaya saw them off easily, killing two North Americans in the process, but his victory was short-lived. Uncle Sam broke diplomatic relations, a move that forced the President to quit.

From then right through the '20s and '30s, US muscle helped to sustain a series of Conservative leaders in Nicaragua. When the first 'free' elections in 1928 put Liberal José Maria Moncada in control, President Herbert Hoover had the excuse he was looking for to scale down America's military presence. Within months the number of marines was reduced from five thousand to around one thousand.

By 1933 the pull-out was complete. Another Liberal, Juan Sacasa, won power and the White House wasted no time in getting the last of the marines home. Such was the haste with which the troops left that it was rumoured that their commanding officer, General Calvin B. Matthews, didn't have time to pack all his personal effects. One of the General's last orders, however, turned out to be his most far-reaching. He appointed an up and coming young Liberal politician called Anastasio Somoza to head up the fledging democracy's Guardia Nacional. At the hand-over a cheerfully confident Somoza promised Matthews: 'I'll give this country peace if I have to shoot every other man in Nicaragua to get it.' If it was a hint of the methods Somoza was prepared to deploy, it was lost on the Marine commander.

Early in 1934 Somoza gave a much clearer illustration of his idea of justice. For many months a guerilla leader called General Augusto Cesar Sandino had been holding out against the new Nicaraguan government. Now that the American forces had left, Sandino wanted peace. He seemed assured of getting his way but he had reckoned without the vengeful nature of the country's security head. On 21st February, 1934 Somoza ordered his Guardia Nacional henchmen to abduct and kill Sandino. Such acts helped feed the later horror stories alleging that he removed enemies by having them hurled kicking and screaming into the heart of the country's active volcano, Masaya.

Now that Somoza had sampled a taste of power it was simply a matter of time before he secured it all. He quickly built up a formidable powerbase in government, earning a reputation as a generous host and a fiery drinker. Alongside his staid uncle, President Sacasa, he seemed a much more natural and ambitious leader. Soon he proved it by seizing complete control.

Sacasa went cap-in-hand to Washington in search of support for a counter-coup, but it was unforthcoming. Hoover had realised the folly of putting young American lives at risk in the turmoil of Central American politics. His policy of strict non-intervention was now being continued by his successor, President Roosevelt. By the end of 1936 Sacasa was in exile and Somoza was the new President.

Over the next twenty years his dictatorship bore all the hall-marks of a love-hate relationship with Washington. He was useful during World War II - the US needed air and naval bases on Nicaraguan soil - but by 1947 it was becoming clear that American foreign policy could not countenance such a blatant despot on its doorstep. Nelson Rockefeller, then Assistant Secretary of State for Inter-American affairs, was despatched to break the news that Somoza's re-election would cause problems for future relations.

Somoza lost no time in naming a puppet successor, 70-year-old Leonardo Arguello, as Liberal presidential candidate for the forthcoming elections. But unfortunately the puppet began cutting the strings by first demanding control of the Guardia Nacional and then calling for Somoza himself to step down. Predictably, he was removed from the candidates' list. Somoza later told a US embassy official: 'Can you imagine? What a stupid bastard. I took him out of Leon where he couldn't earn a dime and he does something crazy like that.'

Under continuing pressure from Washington, Somoza did later hand over the presidency - this time to his elderly uncle, Victor Reyes. But Reyes lasted only a month before he died (of natural causes) and back sprang his nephew to take charge once more.

The early years of the '50s produced some important advances in Nicaragua. Somoza bought new tractors for the grossly inefficient farms, began major land improvement programmes and brought in money-spinning crops such as cotton, rice and coffee. Yet he had a considerable vested interest. By the end of his dictatorship he owned a tenth of all land and had amassed a personal fortune estimated at $60 million, one third more than the country's annual budget.

Somoza loved to give the impression that he was a man of the people and he rarely wasted an opportunity to socialise among them, especially if there were photographers present. What better way to see off his opponents than to show himself as a popular leader. He therefore had no hesitation in accepting an invitation to a party in his honour at the Casa del Obrero workers club in Leon, some fifty miles north of Managua, on the evening of 21st September, 1956. He always said that twenty-one was his lucky number. That night his luck ran out.

Rigoberto Perez, a 27-year-old record salesman who mostly plied his trade across the border in El Salvador, was just one more face in the crowd. He was known among his few friends as a continual, and sometimes boring moaner about the state of the Somoza regime. No-one took much notice. Tonight he knew the Smith and Wesson .38 revolver in his pocket would make them pay more attention.

Tacho, as the people nicknamed Somoza, was sitting among his bodyguards, his distinctive wide-brimmed hat indicating his presence to everyone in the vicinity. He was laughing and joking with his men and had, as usual, been drinking heavily. He didn't notice Perez until the assassin was just a few feet away.

Four shots rang out before the bodyguards sprayed Perez with gunfire, leaving twenty rounds in his body. One smashed into the President's forearm, breaking the bone. Two others lodged in his shoulder. But it was the fourth which brought death to the dicator. It had entered Somoza's bulky frame above the right thigh, penetrating to the base of his spine. He was in enormous pain, but conscious.

Within hours, a team of top US Army doctors, led by President Eisenhower's own surgeon, Major General Leonard D. Heaton, was flying to Leon to assist in the emergency operation. Heaton quickly decided he needed far better medical facilities than those on offer and Somoza was soon en route to Gorgas, Panama, where four surgeons worked for four hours and twenty minutes to remove the bullet close to his spine. It was all in vain. Eight days after he was shot, Anastasio Somoza died of his injuries. For Nicaragua, years of simmering civil war lay ahead.

Somoza's two sons, Luis and Anastasio Junior, took control of Nicaragua before their father died. One of Anastasio Junior's first acts was to round up three thousand 'subversives' for interrogation in the hope of unearthing an assassination conspiracy. He found no evidence and all but three hundred were later released.

The Somoza dynasty finally ended after an earthquake wrecked Managua on 23rd December, 1972. The new Sandinista leadership quickly became a sworn enemy of Washington, which responded by financing and arming two hundred thousand Contra rebels.

John F. Kennedy

John Fitzgerald Kennedy, President of the United States of America, handsome, dashing, charismatic and, at just 46 years of age, the most powerful man in the world, flew into Texas on the morning of 22nd November, 1963 with his beautiful wife, Jackie, at his side. He was anxious about his reception in the Lone Star State. Friends had warned him that his campaign trip there might turn rough. Right-wing Texas was not a place where a liberal President could rely on a warm welcome.

Kennedy wanted to make the best possible entrance into the city of Dallas, where he was to hold a political rally. So, after stepping off US Air Force One at neighbouring Fort Worth Airport, he ordered the bullet-proof Perspex roof of his limousine to be removed so that the crowds would be able to see him more easily. His Secret Service team was horrified; Dallas had one of the highest murder rates in the world and they had already been notified of a number of death threats to the president.

Fears subsided, however, as the presidential motorcade entered the city. It was a hot day and the crowds were out in force. 'Thank you, thank you,' he responded to their clapping and cheering. John F. Kennedy suddenly had good reason to feel buoyant that sunny Friday in Dallas.

By 12.29 pm the open presidential Lincoln was on the city outskirts, five minutes from the venue for the civic lunch which the president was due to attend. The Secret Service agents in the following car felt easier. The crowds were beginning to thin out, and the danger of sniper fire from the city's high office blocks was diminishing.

Ahead loomed a squat, rust-coloured warehouse, the

KENNEDY
ASSASSINATED

A sniper's bullet

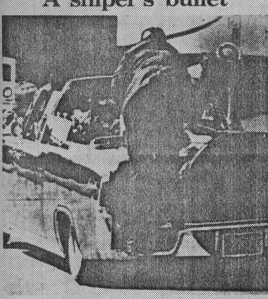

Detective leaps on the rear of President's car as Mrs. Kennedy bends frantically over her shot husband

Seconds after this picture, the President was cradled in her arms

From DAVID ENGLISH
Dallas, Texas, Friday

PRESIDENT KENNEDY was assassinated today by a sniper's bullet as he rode through Dallas in an open car beside his wife Jacqueline.

Cradled in her arms, he was driven to hospital at high speed with motor-cycle sirens screaming ahead.

He was given blood transfusions and operated on—but there was no hope. The surgeon making a cut with tremendous effort found it little too late. Two hours later, he told the President at the head.

He was reported unconscious, the first of several bullets fired into his car and through the head. But then from the head.

He was way in. He was first from unconscious and gone in power with hope beside his second form.

Policeman shot

People were seen holding at a hand of several shots that followed and there were seconds for crowds who standing in a procession standing at a point. He was changed with the assassination.

Several moments that the President may be out driving in a motorcade procession of cars from Dallas Airport into the centre of the city at a speed of twenty time.

Johnson sworn in

World mourning: Page 2
He loved London: Page 3
Photonews: Pages 4 & 5
Man of greatness: Page 8

Killer ate chicken

Continued on Page Two

ARREST
Gunman in cr

Oswald wired - Another pictu

POLICE and F.B.I. men

last tall building on the route: The Texas School Book Depository. Texas Governor John Connally, seated in front of the President, waved to a group of spectators. His wife Nellie turned to Kennedy and said: 'Mr President, you can't say Dallas doesn't love you.'

'That is very obvious,' smiled Kennedy. They were his last words.

The big clock above the book depository now showed 12.30 pm. In front of the building the Lincoln turned left into Dealey Plaza. Green expanses of grass flanked the road.

On a grassy bank to right of the motorcade Dallas dress manufacturer Abraham Zapruder aimed his cine camera at Kennedy as the Lincoln moved away from the depository at eleven miles an hour. For a moment his view of the President was obscured by a road sign. There was a sharp crack.

Some thought it was a firework or a police motorcycle backfiring. As he filmed Kennedy emerging from behind the road sign reaching for his throat, the dumbfounded Zapruder thought that the President was play-acting. But others in Dealey Plaza had instantly recognised the sound as gunfire. Heads swivelled up to the book depository, and several spectators spotted a sniper in a sixth floor window.

Though a bullet had passed through Kennedy's neck, the wound was not fatal. But in the confusion of the moment his Secret Service driver did not react immediately, and for several seconds the powerful Lincoln actually slowed down.

More shots rang out. As Jackie Kennedy turned to her husband, Governor Connally slumped forward with a bullet wound in his chest. Behind, agent Clint Hill jumped from the Secret Service car's running board. Sprinting desperately towards the Lincoln, he saw an explosion of red tear open the President's skull.

With devastating effect, the final bullet had struck home in the most sensational assassination of the century.

Decades later, those six seconds of violence in Dallas remain as intriguing, as murky and as utterly baffling as ever. Was Kennedy assassinated by a lone gunman? Or was he the victim of a conspiracy? Was it a Cuban plot? Did the communists have a hand in it? Or was the killing simply arranged by ultra right-wing Texans?

According to the official Warren Commission assassination report the following year, a 24-year-old book depository employee, Lee Harvey Oswald, operating without accomplices, fired the shots that killed Kennedy. But was Oswald really a lone assassin? Or just a small cog in a carefully planned conspiracy?

Vice-President Lyndon Johnson, who had travelled in the motorcade and was sworn in as President the same afternoon, said in interviews years later that he had always believed more than one person was involved and strongly suspected a communist plot. Because Oswald was a professed Marxist who had once defected to the USSR, Johnson saw in the killing the hand of either Soviet leader Nikita Khrushchev or Cuba's Fidel Castro.

Yet Johnson did not voice these fears at the time. He feared that proof of a communist conspiracy would start a backlash that could conceivably lead the country into war. He almost certainly exerted pressure on the Warren Commission to reach its convenient 'lone nut' verdict. This also suited the FBI and CIA. Both intelligence agencies had Oswald on their files because of his past activities, and they would surely have faced charges of gross incompetence if it were proved that they had failed to detect a major conspiracy involving a left-winger already known to them.

But while the 'lone nut' theory served many interests, it always rang hollow.

According to the commission, Lee Harvey Oswald killed Kennedy with an unknown number of shots fired from the window of a sixth-floor storage area at the Texas Book Depository. Certainly, it was by this window that three spent cartridge cases and a sniper's nest of cardboard boxes were found after the shooting. A rifle lay nearby.

But it is impossible to ignore the unusual activities that occurred at ground level before, during and after the assassination. For it was there, on the so-called grassy knoll roughly a hundred yards from the book depository's sixth floor window, that many investigators believe a second gunman lay in wait.

It was from the grassy mound that Abraham Zapruder, shouting out in horror, shot his historic film of the assassination. Immediately behind the amateur cameraman was a wooden fence which marked the perimeter of Dealey Plaza. It would have made an ideal spot for a second assassin.

Zapruder himself described a shot coming from right behind him which was louder than all the others and reverberated all around him. Of the dozen or so other spectators on the grassy knoll, almost all told a similar story. Four workers from the *Dallas Morning News* spoke of 'a horrible, ear-shattering noise coming from behind us.' Many more people, including secret servicemen, policemen and numerous spectators in or outside the book depository also identified the grassy knoll as a source of gunfire. Of the many policemen who ran to the area, two reported the smell of gunpowder lingering in the bushes beside the perimeter fence.

Just before the shooting, several people had gone behind the fence in search of a good vantage point. A man there had produced a badge, said he was a secret service agent and warned them to move away. Yet at no time, before or after the shooting, were there any secret servicemen in Dealey Plaza, other than those in the motorcade.

Later one of the spectators who had encountered the mystery man described how a shot had come from behind him as the motorcade passed by moments later - so close that he heard it whiz only inches over his left shoulder. Other witnesses spoke of two men running away from the assassination scene onto railway tracks behind the fence. An off-duty policeman saw one man 'slipping and sliding' down the railway embankment into a car park, throw something into the back of a car and speed off. A railway worker whose signal box overlooked the car park described how he saw two strangers by the fence just before the shooting. When the shots were fired he saw 'a flash of light or smoke or something' in the bushes.

So how many gunmen were operating in Dealey Plaza? Governor Connally always rejected the official theory that the bullet which travelled through his chest and wrist and ended up in his thigh was the same one which had passed through Kennedy's neck. He always maintained that he was struck about a second later, and Zapruder's film appears to bear this out. If Connally is right, there must have been more than one gunman firing from the rear, since the rifle found in the depository could not have fired two bullets during such a short space of time.

One firm suspect questioned around this time, following a tip-off that he had been involved in the assassination, was an ex-airline pilot from New Orleans, David Ferrie.

An extreme right-winger who hated Kennedy, Ferrie had for many years been an aide of the rich, ruthless crime boss Carlos Marcello.

David Ferrie had an alibi for the moment of the killing, but investigators have amassed substantial evidence to prove that he knew Oswald. The weekend of the assassination, Ferrie drove hundreds of miles through Texas, apparently in the panic-stricken belief that his library card might be found among Oswald's possessions. In 1966 he was re-questioned in New Orleans following evidence that he had acquired large sums of money just before the assassination. Early in 1967 he was reportedly about to be arrested on suspicion that he had flown one or more assassins out of Dallas in a private aircraft. Just before the arrest, however, he was found dead - officially from natural causes, although he left two typed notes suggesting suicide.

Hours after Ferrie's death the body of his associate Eladio del Valle, also being sought for questioning about the assassination, was found in a car in Miami. Del Valle's skull was split open and he had been shot in the heart. He also had links with crime boss, Marcello.

Despite the probable involvement of other, more powerful conspirators in Kennedy's killing, there can be no reasonable doubt that Lee Harvey Oswald was heavily implicated. The rifle found in the depository was his, and he had brought a long package to work that morning supposedly containing curtain rods.

Oswald was interrogated back in Dallas on 22nd November. Despite the toughness of the questioning and the millions of words that have been written about him since, Oswald remains the most enigmatic figure in the whole story of the assassination.

Killing field of fire: The Dallas Book Depository and the grassy knoll.

A mass of contradictions, he was cunning, purposeful, of above average intelligence, yet strangely naive. At 16 he was apparently fascinated by Communism, yet was determined to join one of the great symbols of American patriotism, the US Marines. Despite making no secret of his left-wing stance, he was posted to a top-secret US air base in Japan which housed U-2 spy planes. Despite his access to military secrets, no-one appears to have objected when he applied to travel to Russia, where he immediately renounced his US citizenship and stayed for two years.

There is a plausible case to be made for his defection having been an elaborate charade organised by US military intelligence. Certainly Oswald had no trouble getting back into the States, accompanied by his Russian wife, when he became 'fed up' with the USSR two years later.

In 1963 he moved to New Orleans (Carlos Marcello's centre of operations) and became actively involved in left-wing politics, espousing the cause of Cuba's new communist dictator, Fidel Castro. Yet at the same time he was also apparently mixing with men of the extreme right.

In October that same year he moved to Dallas - by which time Kennedy's visit there had already been announced - and took a job at the book depository. Then, on 22nd November, the man who had never been heard to express anything but admiration for President Kennedy became the chief suspect in his killing.

After the assassination, things quickly went wrong for Oswald.

One of the first policemen to dash into the depository moments after the shooting found him calmly sipping Coca-Cola in the second-floor lunch-room. Within minutes, however, he had fled the scene. He went by bus and taxi to his lodgings, changed clothes, then set off up the road on foot.

Some fifteen minutes later, about a mile from Oswald's lodgings, there was yet another killing. Police patrolman J.D. Tippit stopped his car to speak to a man on the pavement. The man pulled out a pistol, gunned him down and ran off.

The Warren Commission ruled that Oswald, presumably fearing he was about to be picked up for Kennedy's murder, was Tippit's killer.

It is possible that a panic-stricken Oswald did indeed shoot Tippit. But it remains a puzzling incident. At the time, police had circulated only the briefest of descriptions of the sniper seen at the window: 'White male, approximately 30 years old, 165 pounds, slender build.' It could have fitted tens of thousands of Dallas inhabitants. Why did Tippit want to speak to this particular man?

Shortly after Tippit's death, a shopkeeper saw Oswald go into a cinema, thought he looked suspicious and called the police, who arrested him after a struggle. By the afternoon of the assassination, everything was pointing to Oswald's guilt - perhaps just as had been planned.

In custody, Oswald repeatedly denied that he had shot either Kennedy or Tippit and claimed several times that he had been set up. 'I'm just a patsy,' he kept saying.

But a patsy for whom? If Oswald were about to justify his claim, he would need to be silenced. Enter night-club owner Jack Ruby.

For millions of Americans, the shooting of Oswald by Ruby two days later was the final proof of a conspiracy. Yet the Warren Commission insisted that Ruby had acted quite independently, that he impulsively walked into Dallas Police HQ at the precise moment when Oswald was being led to a car to transfer him to jail and killed him to avenge Jackie Kennedy. That conclusion sounds even more feeble today than it did then.

Soon after Oswald's arrest, Ruby had made a monumental number of telephone calls. And, like David Ferrie, he suddenly became flush with money. Though usually in debt, he was seen in his bank on the afternoon of the assassination carrying $7,000 in cash.

He also started showing an obsessive interest in Oswald. At 7 pm that night he managed to open a door to the room where Oswald was being interrogated, and was told to move on by a policeman who knew him. Later that night he was present at a press conference at which Oswald was briefly paraded, and he was back again the next day trying to find out when Oswald was to be transferred.

It now seems certain he finally got his way by bribing a police officer to slip him past the heavy security at the crucial moment.

But it is Ruby's background, glossed over by the Warren Commission, that adds a sinister twist. He was, in fact, a minor figure in the Mafia who, according to FBI documents, had for years been a pay-off man for the Dallas Police Department. But the man to whom he was probably ultimately responsible was Mafia boss Carlos Marcello of New Orleans.

Ruby maintained until his death in jail in 1967 of cancer that he had been duped into killing Oswald. But at least he died peacefully. Others were not so lucky.

One of the alarming features of the assassination is the chain of murders, accidents and apparent suicides left in its wake. Quite apart from Oswald himself, and men like David Ferrie and his associate Eladio del Valle, many key witnesses died suddenly and violently.

Three newspaper reporters who spoke to Ruby about

the Kennedy case also died in rapid succession, one from a gunshot wound, one from a karate chop and the third from a drug overdose. Three Mafia men were murdered shortly after a new government inquiry team asked to see them. Another important witness was found shot dead two hours after learning that Congressional investigators wanted to question him about his links with Oswald.

The Congressional Committee finally came up with its findings - several theories but few conclusions - in 1979. One theory to which they gave strong credence was that Kennedy's death was a direct result of his Cuban policy.

Following the 1961 Bay of Pigs invasion in which exiled anti-Castro Cubans, trained by the CIA and backed by Kennedy, landed on Cuba in a disastrously bungled coup attempt, the severely embarrassed President slowly began back-pedalling in his attitude to Castro. By 1963, in the wake of the Cuban missile crisis, he was making it clear that he wanted operations against Castro stopped. The anti-Castro Cubans were furious - furious enough, some think, to turn against Kennedy and plot to kill him.

Here, of course, they might have found willing allies in Mafia men like Carlos Marcello and his fellow crime boss, Santos Trafficante, whose lucrative gambling and prostitution empire on Cuba had crumbled after Castro's takeover.

Both Marcello and Trafficante loathed John Kennedy and his brother Robert. Both were suffering under the relentless crusade against organised crime initiated by Robert Kennedy, as Attorney-General, with Jack's blessing. The Kennedy brothers were pursuing the Mafia as never before, and the Mafia's multi-billion dollar empire was under serious threat.

To his undying fury, Marcello was deported on Robert

Kennedy's orders. On his return, say associates, the proud Sicilian swore revenge. One chilling conversation between Marcello and three colleagues in late 1962 was described to the Congressional Assassination Committee. Referring to the Kennedys, he said: 'The dog will keep biting you if you only cut off its tail.' He clearly believed that, with John Kennedy dead, Robert Kennedy would cease to be Attorney-General - a correct assumption. He even spoke of 'setting up a nut to take the blame.' It was at about this time too that Trafficante reportedly told an associate: 'The President is going to be hit.'

In 1979 the Congressional Committee felt sufficiently confident to declare that elements of the Mafia were behind Kennedy's killing. It added that the most likely family bosses of organised crime to have participated were Carlos Marcello and Santos Trafficante, both of whom had the motive, means and opportunity.

But, as with every other theory in the vilest assassination of the century, there was no proof. The murder of John Fitzgerald Kennedy remains one of the murkiest mysteries of all time.

Malcolm X

American blacks were hard-up, fed up and badly in need of a hero. Malcolm X seemed like the answer to their prayers. Outspoken and extreme, he struck a different chord to the conciliatory black leaders emerging at the time, notably Martin Luther King. King was a peace-maker. Malcolm X urged violence to fight white supremacy, to the delight of many of the angry, frustrated young blacks.

His radical words won many hearts and minds. Yet although he had plenty of political know-how, he found it impossible to curb his tongue. Malcolm X ended up with enemies not only amongst the anxious whites but also amongst the black population. Finally, even some of his own supporters had had their fill. There were plenty of people who wanted him dead. They would not be disappointed.

Born Malcolm Little in Omaha, Nebraska, in 1926, he was the son of a baptist minister. From the cradle he was spoon-fed the case for black nationalism. His father was a follower of the Marcus Garvey 'Back to Africa' movement. He was only a tot when he learned the sorry story of black suffering in America.

In 1929 he and his family moved to Lansing, Michigan, but, being coloured, they found no welcome awaiting them. Racists set fire to their new home. As flames engulfed the walls of their house, young Malcolm surely knew the battle lines were drawn.

When Malcolm was 6, his father died, apparently the victim of a road accident. Yet suspiciously, the body was covered with bruises. Malcolm was convinced that the

Malcolm X preached a creed of violent revolution -
and died a violent death.

official explanation for the death of his activist father was intended to fob off himself and the rest of the family. He firmly believed that his beloved father had been beaten up by whites and dumped on the road.

As a teenager, he decided to make his mark and it was none too pleasant. He drifted between Boston and New York, first working as a waiter but then degenerating into petty crime. He was a pimp, drug pusher, hustler and thief. When the law finally caught up with him at just 18 years of age, he was jailed for ten years.

It was during the jail term that he realised the world of ghetto crime for young blacks was overcrowded and unrewarding. Education was the way ahead, he decided, and he drank in the words of heavy-weight books as once he might have knocked back beer. Behind bars, he realised that, when he spoke, people listened. He worked to improve his oratory powers, determined that, when he was on the outside again, he would make a difference.

His imagination was captured by the Black Muslim sect led by Elijah Muhammed. Here was a philosophy of anti-white sentiment to which Malcolm could relate. There was no appeasement of whites in the movement, only antagonism. When he was released from jail in 1952 he lent his full weight to the Black Muslims, gladly giving up the surname which white slave traders had awarded his family years before. Malcolm also adopted the lifestyle of a dedicated Muslim which meant no drinking, smoking or pre-marital sex. He married a Muslim woman, Betty Shibazz, and became an assistant minister in Muslim Temple No. 1, in Detroit.

By now it was impossible to ignore him. Physically, he bore few credentials of a great black leader. He wore horn-rimmed spectacles and was pale of skin - his maternal grandmother had been raped by a white man.

Yet his words were electrifying. People flocked to hear his message which was savagely anti-white. Like many of his fellow blacks, he was tired of waiting for equal rights which were long overdue in arriving. He had little patience for the peaceable campaign being orchestrated by Martin Luther King, which he saw as nothing more than 'Uncle Tomism' - a parody of blacks by blacks. With a characteristically direct approach, he urged violence instead of votes and bullets instead of ballots.

When a plane crash killed scores of white people, he openly rejoiced at the news. He even expressed satisfaction at the assassination of President John F. Kennedy in 1963. By now he was in charge of the Muslim's temple in New York and a challenger for the leadership of the movement, renamed the Nation of Islam.

Elijah Muhammad and his successor and son-in-law Raymond Sharrief were far from pleased. Malcolm put them in the shade and they knew it. They were impatient to oust him. His insensitive comments about President Kennedy gave them the opportunity they had been looking for.

Malcolm was suspended from the Nation of Islam. In reply, he formed his own army, the Organisation of Afro-American Unity. He turned the full force of his expert eloquence and vitriol against his former friends. Not content with going it alone, he accused Elijah Muhammad of all sorts of immoral behaviour and even of collaborating with the hateful Ku Klux Klan.

The movement was thoroughly divided. Two of Elijah's own sons defected to Malcolm's side, adding salt to an open and festering wound. In his mouthpiece newspaper called *Muhammad Speaks* Elijah wrote: 'Only those who wish to be led to hell or to their doom will follow Malcolm. The die is set and Malcolm shall not escape.'

Yet Malcolm had yet to prove what a true enigma he really was. During a five week trip to Mecca, the holiest place in Islam, his views suddenly mellowed. Gone was the merciless hostility towards whites. In its place was a more reasoned attitude, comparable to that which existed in King's movement.

Now militants in his own movement turned against him, as well as angry members of the Nation of Islam. Malcolm believed that he was mostly at risk from his former colleagues in the Nation of Islam. 'I'm a marked man,' he admitted in an interview given just weeks before his death.

'It doesn't frighten me for myself as long as I felt they would not hurt my family. No-one can get out without trouble and this thing with me will be resolved by death and violence.'

'I was the spokesman for the Black Muslims. I believed in Elijah Muhammad more strongly than Christians do in Jesus. I believed in him so strongly that my mind, my body, my voice functioned 100 per cent for him and the movement. My belief led others to believe. Now I'm out. And there's the fear if my image isn't shattered the Muslims in the movement will leave. Then, they know I know a lot.'

If he was in any doubt about the danger he was in, it was spelled out for him in February, 1965, when a fire-bomb destroyed his home in Queens, New York.

Just a week later, Malcolm was speaking before an audience of four hundred at a mosque in Harlem. A hush fell as he rose to address the audience, separated from them by a small army of bodyguards. He had barely begun when a disturbance broke out at the front. A man stood up yelling: 'Get your hand off my pockets. Don't be messing with my pockets.'

Bodyguards rushed towards him, but Malcolm tried to soothe the situation by saying: 'Now brothers, be cool.' Yet even as he spoke, a smoke bomb erupted from the rear of the hall. In the confusion, a gunman seized his chance. He strode towards the stage through the centre of the mosque, produced a sawn-off shotgun and blasted Malcolm in the chest.

It was the signal for two further gunmen to emerge. They rushed forward, armed with handguns, and pumped more bullets into the body which lay bleeding on the podium.

The assassin armed with a shotgun was himself shot by a bodyguard. Despite a leg wound, he continued to make his escape until an angry crowd descended on him outside, battering him by way of revenge. It was the police who pulled him to safety from the pavement. The other two fled the scene.

Malcolm was rushed to the nearby Columbia Presbyterian Medical Centre straight into an operating theatre. It was there that he died, aged only 39. His distraught wife, Betty, who had witnessed the terrible scene, was pregnant with their fifth child.

In police custody was Talmage Hayer, otherwise known as Thomas Hagan. He was a 22-year-old father of two who confounded the police investigation because nothing linked him to the Nation of Islam, widely thought to be responsible for Malcolm's death. Supporters of Malcolm needed no convincing about who was to blame. A Black Muslim temple was burnt out two days later.

Detectives later arrested Black Muslim members Norman 3X (Butler) and Thomas 15X (Johnson) and all three were convicted of the murder. Little heed was paid to Hayer, who strenuously denied that Norman and Thomas were involved, or to Elijah Muhammad, who declared his movement and its members innocent.

The defence that Norman had received hospital treatment that morning for a disabling condition on his right leg also counted for nothing. Blacks were convinced that the police operation had been a shoddy one and that both men arrested afterwards were innocent.

Malcolm was buried in Fercliff Cemetry as a Muslim, white robed and facing east towards Mecca. His gravestone bears the name Al Hajj Malik Shabazz. Three gunmen, whatever their identities, removed from the American political scene one of its fieriest revolutionaries.

Martin Luther King

He was a man with a dream, and to Black America in the mid 1960s that dream was freedom. Black people in their millions looked to Dr Martin Luther King as their true leader, not some white President in Washington. They devoured his speeches and they flooded onto the streets for his protests. King, they believed, was the man who would give them a voice.

As an ordained Baptist minister and superb preacher, he was comfortable in his unofficial role as America's leading civil rights activist. His insistence on non-violent protests, such as sit-ins, won him enormous publicity, while at the same time frustrating his enemies. And there were many of those.

Southern whites hated him for trying to change the status quo which had been in force since the days of slavery. Right-wingers hated him for his outspoken condemnation of the Vietnam War. FBI director, J. Edgar Hoover, hated him for both reasons - plus the fact that he had won the 1964 Nobel Peace Prize. Inevitably, thousands of racists hated him because he was an intelligent, well-educated, successful black man.

King was exceptionally intelligent. At the age of 5 he could recite lengthy passages from the Bible and could sing the longest hymn from memory. At 15 he was allowed to skip his final year at senior school and headed straight for Atlanta's Morehouse College, where he graduated in 1947 with a sociology degree and a fierce ambition to join the ministry. He obtained a top BA in divinity at Crozer Theological Seminary in Pennsylvania and completed his education at Boston University in 1955 with a Ph.D in sys-

Martin Luther King: The prophet of peace, tragically gunned down.

tematic theology. He married fellow Boston student Coretta Scott, also a committed civil rights campaigner, who later give birth to his four children.

King's greatest influences as a student were the Indian leader, Mahatma Gandhi, the American poet David Thoreau, and the preacher-sociologist Walter Rauschenbusch. Of these, Gandhi was the one who gave his life a new purpose. He realised that civil disobedience could be a powerful weapon with which to fight injustice. He still felt anger at the treatment of blacks, but now it was a controlled anger. Soon it would rock the American Establishment to the core.

His first victory came in November, 1956. King had been assigned to the Dexter Avenue Baptist Church in Montgomery, Alabama, and for almost a year he had been leading a campaign by Montgomery blacks to end racial segregation on buses. For the first time his rolling baritone voice was heard across America and it captivated millions.

Alabama's racist segregation law was torn up by the United States Supreme Court and King was hailed as the saviour of Black America. White extremist terrorists responded by blowing up his house while it was empty - a move that completely backfired on them. The storm was gathering and soon it would sweep away much of the old regime.

Throughout the early and mid '60s, King challenged the system which oppressed blacks at every opportunity. The violence with which police treated his marches was re-played on television screens and in newspapers around the world, causing uproar on Capitol Hill. Far from being an overnight sensation, US politicians saw that King's power base was increasing by the day. To a critical public it was the preacher who seemed to be in control, making the police look like a disorganised rabble.

In 1963 he delivered his famous 'I have a dream' speech to over two hundred thousand enthralled supporters at the Lincoln Memorial in Washington DC. By 1964 a Civil Rights Act was in place. The following year saw the Federal Voting Rights Act, which for the first time guaranteed blacks the vote. And all the time the civil rights movement was growing. Other black leaders joined the cause: Malcolm X, Huey Newton, Eldridge Cleaver. However, their commitment to more aggressive ways of reforming injustice was anathema to King. He stuck by his philosophy of non-violent civil disobedience.

Over the years, the FBI head, Hoover, had grown increasingly angry and frustrated at King's activities. Hoover saw him as a devious agitator, whose reputation as a womaniser meant that he failed to practise what he preached. For years Hoover's men hounded King, secretly monitoring his phone conversations, infiltrating his Southern Christian Leadership movement and spreading propaganda about his private life. The FBI even had a special task force, whose job was to tarnish King's reputation. One memo which these officers received from Hoover included the instruction to 'remove (King) from the national scene.'

On 3rd April, 1968 King arrived in Memphis, Tennessee, to address a meeting of two thousand supporters. His last visit to the city a few days earlier had resulted in widespread street violence. He had been heading a march in support of striking city sanitation workers when trouble erupted at the tail of the demo. One teenager had died, sixty people were hurt and more than two hundred were arrested.

The 39-year-old King received numerous death threats

following the incident. Typically he refused to back down. At a sermon in Memphis the following day he said: 'Every now and then I guess we all think realistically about that day when we will all be victimised with what is life's final common denominator, that something we call death. We all think about it and every now and then I think about my own funeral. And I don't think about it in the morbid sense. And every now and then I ask myself what it is that I would want said, and I leave word for you this morning .... I won't have any money to leave behind. I won't have the fine and luxurious things to leave behind. But what I do want to do is to leave a committed life behind and that is all I want to say.'

That afternoon he returned to the Lorraine Motel in Memphis and settled down in room 305. On the other side of the street was a run-down doss house. In room 5 a drifter and convicted armed robber called James Earl Ray, on the run from the Missouri state prison, was psyching himself up to kill.

Ray was a man with a Jekyll and Hyde personality. Some who knew him spoke of a reserved, modest man who shunned alcohol and quietly got on with the business of life. Others told of a hard-drinking, foul-mouthed racist. In Memphis that day, Ray the racist was in control and Martin Luther King was the subject of his hate. There is a theory that Ray's hatred of black people dated from his childhood when he discovered that his family home had been sold to a black family. The rise of Martin Luther King gave his twisted mind the perfect target for revenge.

On the afternoon of 4th April, Ray picked up the 30.06 Remington pump-action rifle which he had bought two days earlier and moved to the bathroom above his room - his chosen position for the assassination of Martin Luther

King. Several times Ray shouldered the rifle and peered through the telescopic sight at a man moving around inside room 305. But he could never be certain that the man was King.

Finally, at about 6 pm, his moment came. King appeared on the balcony dressed in a black suit in readiness for the evening rally. He leaned over the railing to shout down at one of his young aides, Jesse Jackson, urging him to go and get dressed for dinner. Behind him another colleague, Dr Ralph Abernathy, was preparing to walk out onto the balcony.

Above them Ray squeezed the trigger and a mini explosion stopped Abernathy in mid-stride. King clutched his throat and then sank to the floor with blood pumping from the right side of his neck. His tie had been blown away in the impact of the dum-dum bullet before it smashed through his spinal cord. Aides rushed to his side, pressing towels against the wound in a futile attempt to stem the flow of blood.

King was still alive when they wheeled him onto the operating table at nearby St Joseph Hospital, but by 7.05 pm he was dead. His last words before the fatal shot rang out had been to ask a musician at Jesse Jackson's side to play a particular song at the evening rally. The song was *Precious Lord, Take My Hand*. 'I really want you to play that tonight,' said King.

It took Earl only minutes to make his getaway. The assassination set off one of the biggest manhunts America had ever seen, as FBI agents tried to pinpoint the killer's movements and unravel the tangle of false identities that he left in his wake.

Meanwhile black communities across the nation were rising up in protest at what many believed was a government sponsored execution. There were nine thousand troops on the streets of Washington and a 4 pm curfew. Stores were looted in in Detroit, Boston and New York. And in Chicago seven blacks were killed in two nights of rioting which resulted in six thousand National Guard troopers patrolling the city.

Still nothing was heard of Ray. The FBI knew some of his aliases: Paul Bridgeman, Ramon George Sneyd, Eric Galt and John Willard (the name he'd used to check in to the Memphis doss house). But they had no firm leads. Then suddenly investigators got a couple of breaks. A single fingerprint found in a room rented by Eric Galt was identified as that of escaped convict James Earl Ray. It matched the prints on the rifle he'd left behind in Memphis. At last they had a name and a face.

On 17th May the hunt came to a dramatic end in London. Scotland Yard detectives had already passed information to the FBI advising that Ray had stopped in England temporarily en route to Portugal. He had been trying to enlist as a mercenary with Angolan or Rhodesian forces. Now an alert officer at Heathrow airport had stopped a man travelling under the Canadian passport of Ramon George Sneyd. His fingerprints were wired to FBI headquarters. Within hours moves were underway to extradite James Earl Ray for trial.

Ray was later convicted of murder and sentenced to ninety-nine years. He pleaded guilty but claimed he was only a pawn in a conspiracy of faceless right-wing extremists. Many people felt that there could be some truth in his claim. Where did a small-time crook get the know-how to pick aliases and obtain the passports of men he resembled? Where did he get the money to travel to Europe? Why did he take such care to leave a bundle of evidence - including

Assassin's target: Martin Luther King, accompanied by aides Jesse Jackson and Dr. Ralph Abernathy, at his Memphis motel the day before he was shot.

the rifle covered with fingerprints - behind him?

The conspiracy theories rage to this day. If there were others behind the assassination of Martin Luther King, they clearly wanted to halt civil rights reform, keep Black America at the bottom of the pile and strike a far-reaching blow for the cause of white supremacy.

They failed. Even in death, King's inspirational teachings continue to focus the struggle for true black equality.

Robert Kennedy

Just as everyone old enough can remember exactly what they were doing at the time Jack Kennedy was assassinated, so can they recall the words they uttered a few years later when his younger brother, Robert, was gunned down: 'Oh no, not again.'

Bobby Kennedy had just won the California Democratic presidential primary on 5th June, 1968, when he was shot to death in a kitchen corridor of the Ambassador Hotel in Los Angeles. His brother, Jack, had been 43 when he was murdered in Dallas. Bobby was just 42.

Like his brother, Jack, Robert Kennedy was a leading Liberal. Like his brother, he had fought corruption in government and the unions, and had battled organised crime in the community. Like him, he had made many powerful enemies. Like him, he was hated by the die-hard American right wing. Like his brother, he paid the ultimate price for his courageous defiance.

Bobby Kennedy's decision to follow in his brother's footsteps and run for the Democratic nomination for President of the United States was taken in the full knowledge of the terrible risks of that role. He had alienated the far right by his support of the civil rights movement. He had infuriated the trade union bosses by his clampdown on their money laundering rackets. And, as Attorney General, he had made enemies of the Mafia godfathers.

Towards midnight on 4th June, 1968 the youthful presidential hopeful made a speech to his supporters in the ballroom of the Ambassador Hotel, where he was staying during the campaign. He paid tribute to his wife, Ethel,

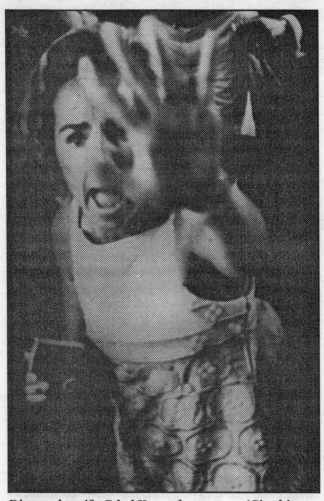

Distraught wife, Ethel Kennedy, screams: 'Give him air, give him air!'

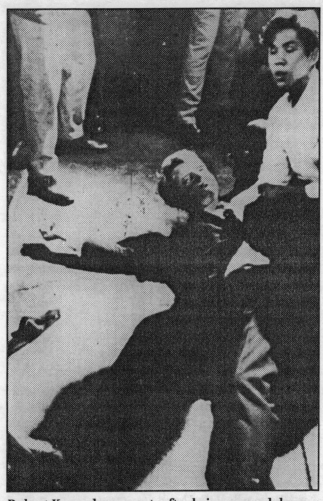

Robert Kennedy moments after being gunned down in a Los Angeles hotel.

and told the cheering Democrats: 'We are a great country, an unselfish country and a compassionate country. I intend to make that the basis for running as President.'

Later he quickly washed and changed, and then set out through the corridors of the Ambassador to the meeting room where he was to hold an early morning press conference. Surrounded by his advisors and few unarmed security men, he suddenly took a short cut through the hotel's kitchens. Waiting for him in a narrow passageway was Sirhan Bishara Sirhan.

The young Arab rushed forward, pulled a pistol from his clothes and fired two shots at point blank range. The first shot from Sirhan's .22 calibre Iver Johnson pistol went through Kennedy's shoulder. He would have survived that one. But a second bullet crashed into his skull and he hit the floor. It was 12.13 am.

Sirhan kept firing as hotel employees wrestled him to the ground. Unlike his murdered brother, Bobby did not die instantly. Rushed to hospital, doctors announced: 'His pulse came back and we began to hear a heartbeat. Then he began to breathe erratically.' At 1.45 am, however, he was dead.

Sirhan Bishara Sirhan was a 24-year-old Palestinian who had entered the US as an immigrant at the age of 12. His parents had split up and he lived with his two brothers in Pasadena, California. Found in his apartment was a statement that he planned to murder Robert Kennedy 'before 5th June, 1968' - the first anniversary of the Six Day War, in which the United States had supported Israel against its Arab foes. Sirhan pleaded guilty to murder and was sentenced to the electric chair. In 1970 California banned the death penalty and he began a life sentence in San Quentin prison.

Since the murder of Bobby Kennedy happened just two months after the assassination of civil rights leader, Martin Luther King, several investigators have linked the two killings with that of John F. Kennedy in 1963 - and produced the most widespread conspiracy theories of all. Most Americans, however, see the shooting of Robert Kennedy as just a sick and savage copycat killing.

Aldo Moro

In the tangle of post-war Italian politics, of shifting coalitions and sporadic general elections, one man stood out above the inter-party chaos.

Aldo Moro was an honoured and respected politician who had led both the country's Christian Democratic Party and the national government. It was probably for this reason that he was marked out for kidnap and assassination by urban terrorist fanatics. Although he had stood down from power, he was a symbol of the system they hated.

A few minutes after 9 am on Sunday, 16th March, 1978 Moro was driving home from early mass at the church which he attended regularly. Suddenly a car bearing diplomatic licence plates and driven by a man in an airline uniform drew alongside, taking Moro's driver by surprise and forcing him off the road.

A second car screeched to a halt, followed by a third. Five men and a woman leapt out, firing machine guns from the hip. Moro's driver and bodyguard were killed before they could react, as were three security men in a car that always shadowed Moro's. Moro himself was hauled from his seat and thrust into one of the ambush vehicles, in which he was driven away at high speed. The attack was all over within three minutes.

Police were still picking over the clues at the scene of the ambush when Aldo Moro's kidnappers telephoned a press agency and identified themselves as a unit of the Red Brigade, a murderous army of disaffected Communists, political and social misfits and thugs who terrorised Italy for a number of unhappy years. They had been responsible for countless atrocities in the country over a period of more

Aldo Moro, the respected Italian kidnapped by the infamous Red Brigade.

than a decade.

A massive search was soon underway, led by Italian anti-terrorist police and assisted by a German specialist team and members of the British Army's elite SAS. For several weeks these teams set about picking up known Red Brigade sympathisers and left-wing activists, without getting any closer to their goal.

Meanwhile, the kidnap gang was putting out regular communiqués to the press, outlining the terms for the release of Signor Moro. These were the usual mixture of Marxist dogma and threats of violence. They stated that Moro was being interrogated 'to clarify the imperialist and anti-proletarian policies of the Christian Democrats and to pinpoint precisely the international structures and national affiliations of the imperialist counter-revolutionaries.'

The Italian government announced at the outset that there would be no deals or negotiations with the terrorists, and they received all-party support for their stance. However, as the weeks passed, the messages from the Red Brigade became ever more threatening. On 15th April they announced that Moro had been tried by a 'people's court' and sentenced to death 'for the evil complicity of his regime in the bloodiest pages of the history of recent years.' Three days later came another communiqué saying that Moro had committed suicide and his body would be found in Lake Duchessa in the Apennine mountains north of Rome. A huge search revealed nothing.

Two days after that came another message that Moro was still alive but that he would be executed within forty-eight hours unless a number of Communist prisoners were released from jail. But on 18th April there had been a breakthrough for the authorities when they found a Red Brigade hideout on the outskirts of Rome, containing

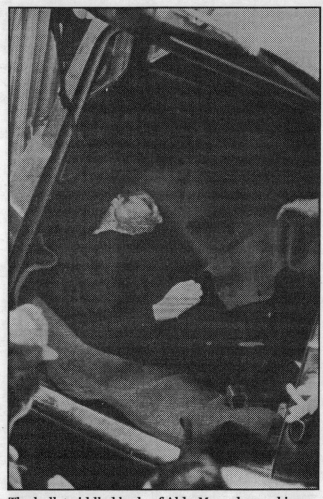

The bullet-riddled body of Aldo Moro dumped in a parked car in central Rome.

weapons, airline uniforms and diplomatic car plates. It had been, until recently, Signor Moro's prison.

By this time, the Moro family and the Christian Democrats were wavering from the official 'no deals' line. On 3rd May they urged the government to seek a compromise. It was too late. The terrorists had either run out of patience or lost their nerve.

On 5th May the kidnappers announced: 'The battle begun on 16th March with the capture of Aldo Moro has now reached its conclusion. The only language the imperialist lackeys have shown they understand is the language of the gun.'

That same day, Signor Moro's wife received a farewell letter from her husband, in which he wrote: 'They are going to kill me in a little while.'

On 9th May the Red Brigade called police and warned them of a car bomb outside the Christian Democrat headquarters building. A bomb disposal unit dispatched to the scene found no explosives ... but the body of Aldo Moro stuffed in the boot. He had been shot in the head eleven times earlier that morning.

A week later - a week too late - police raided a Red Brigade printing works in Rome and arrested five extremists. These five, along with fifty-eight others, were charged with murder or complicity in the kidnapping of Signor Moro, and most received long jail sentences.

Georgi Ivanov Markov

It was the kind of thing that happens every day. A crowded street, a touch by a stranger, a muttered apology. But in the case of Georgi Ivanov Markov, the touch was the touch of death.

Georgi Markov, a Bulgarian dissident living in exile in London, had fled from his communist homeland in 1969. A playwright, he had quarrelled with the authorities and taken his beliefs to the free world. He was never free, however, of the regime that regarded any desire for liberty as a threat.

Markov married an English woman and worked for the BBC's World Service. And while his broadcasts were beamed to Eastern Europe, his personal contributions were not violently political. He had nothing to fear from the Communist regime he had fled. Or so he thought.

Early in the evening of Wednesday, 7th September, 1978 he was walking from his Bush House workplace in London's Aldwych to the car that he had parked on the other side of the River Thames. The area is one that is thronged with people at almost every hour of the day, as it is in the vicinity of theatreland, Australia House, the London School of Economics, several big hotels and a number of government buildings, including the massive Somerset House. To the west is the tourist hub of London and to the east lies Fleet Street, leading to the City and the nation's business capital.

Hardly the place for a dramatic - and still unexplained - assassination. Yet as Markov walked past a bus queue on the busy Aldwych, he was prodded in the thigh by the tip of an umbrella. The man holding it apologised briefly, then

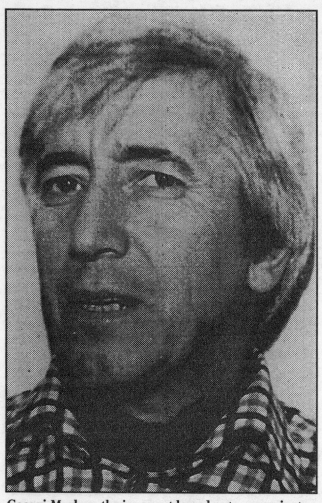

Georgi Markov, the innocent broadcaster assassinated on a London street.

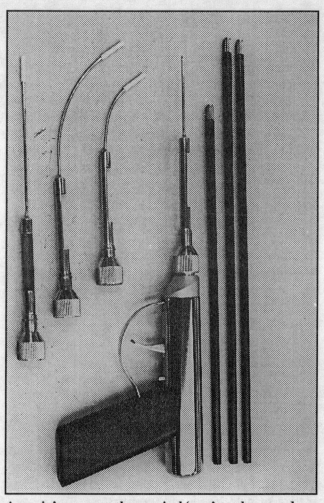

Assassin's weapon: the surgical 'gun' used to murder
Georgi Markov.

hailed a taxi and was gone. He had a strong east European accent.

Markov returned to Bush House after moving his car closer to his place of work. He did not even notice the tiny cut in his leg where the umbrella had pierced the skin. He did some translating, read a news bulletin and returned home. The next day he was off duty, and he was scheduled to return to Bush House on the Friday. He never made it.

The following day he was running a fever and asked his wife, Annabel, to ring the BBC to warn them that they should get cover for his shift. By Friday morning he was so ill that he was admitted to St James's Hospital in Balham, South London, where his sickness baffled doctors.

It was Markov himself who supplied the answer. He had realised that the prod with the umbrella was not as innocent as he had at first thought. He believed that he had been the target of a communist assassin. The doctors he told this to were dumbfounded, but nevertheless informed the police. Before the police could interview Markov, however, he had slipped into a coma. He never regained consciousness.

A post-mortem failed to establish the cause of death. A body tissue sample was sent to Scotland Yard's forensic laboratories, but this too drew a blank. Finally a sample went to Porton Down, Wiltshire, the Government's chemical weapons research station. Results of the analysis were never made public, yet suddenly Scotland Yard's anti-terrorist squad and MI5 were called in. They interviewed Markov's family, friends and associates.

They discovered that Markov's life had been threatened six months earlier. Markov's publisher, David Farrer, revealed that the dissident had told him that a Bulgarian stranger had called on him, carrying a letter of introduction from a German friend. According to what Markov told Farrer, the Bulgarian had had a few drinks with Markov, then had declared: 'I've been sent here to kill you. But I'm not going to do it. I'll take the money and go.'

Markov had apparently been disturbed, but still had not felt that anyone would make an attempt at murder in the heart of London. He could not have been more wrong.

The Government, now convinced that Markov had been murdered in James Bond style, confronted the Bulgarians. Predictably they denied any complicity in Markov's death. Suggestions that their secret services had been involved were described as 'absurd'.

Police investigations failed to reveal the identity of the mysterious stranger with the umbrella. Nevertheless, the case was effectively closed, as the murder itself had ceased to be a mystery. Markov had been killed by the injection into his thigh of a pellet of ricin, a poisonous derivative of the bean of the castor oil plant, *Ricinus Sanguineus*.

Mrs Annabel Markov never gave up her campaign for some measure of justice. She unsuccessfully campaigned for a public enquiry into her husband's death. Only in 1991, following the collapse of the discredited communist regime in Bulgaria, did the new government admit its country's guilt over Markov's death.

Even so, the Aldwych umbrella assassin has still not been brought to book.

Lord Louis Mountbatten

Among the younger members of the British Royal Family, Lord Louis Mountbatten was a hero figure. He was a man whose laughing eyes and mischievous sense of humour would enrich any occasion, whose war record proved he was a cut above most of his peers and whose common sense was valued by royals and politicians alike. To Prince Charles and Prince Andrew especially, the man they knew as 'Uncle Dickie' seemed almost blessed with immortality.

Perhaps, in a way, Mountbatten had come to share that view. He had been through so many scrapes in his distinguished military career that it was never his tendency to worry about personal safety. It was part of the strength of his character. It was also his fatal mistake.

For thirty-five years he had spent an annual summer holiday at his imposing, stone-turreted castle close to the fishing community of Mullaghmore in north-west Ireland. He loved the rugged cliffs and the green hills as much as he loved the local people. And they took to him because he was never aloof or haughty like other members of the aristocracy. Local children were regularly invited to join him for day trips in his fishing smack, 'Shadow V', while professional fishermen enjoyed bantering with him along the quay or in the local pub.

Yet this was Ireland, a nation torn apart by the hatred between extremist Protestants in the North and extremist Republicans in the South. Leading the Republican struggle was the Army Council of the Provisional Irish Republican Army. To them, the British government was an occupying power and any representative of it could be treated as a

Louis Mountbatten: the young 'Uncle Dickie', favourite of the Royal Family.

Setting sail in 'Shadow V', the boat later targeted by Irish terrorist bombers.

legitimate target. Mountbatten of Burma, last Viceroy of India, Admiral of the Fleet, second cousin to the Queen, uncle of Prince Philip and leading pillar of the British establishment, fulfilled all their requirements for a headline-making assassination.

There were other reasons, too, why the IRA wanted him dead that sunny day - 27th August, 1979. First and foremost, they needed the kudos of a high-profile killing to match the success of their deadly rivals within the Republican movement, the Irish National Liberation Army. The previous year this splinter group had pulled off a major coup by blowing up the senior Conservative MP, Airey Neave, inside the grounds of the Houses of Parliament.

Secondly, 1979 marked the ten-year anniversary of British troops on the streets of Northern Ireland. Such a milestone, it was decided, should be marked in blood. Finally, there was the cynical thirst for publicity. By carrying out the murder ahead of the bank holiday weekend - a quiet time for the news media - they could guarantee non-stop coverage for days on television and in the newspapers.

The danger in which Mountbatten placed himself during his Mullaghmore holidays was recognised by the Sligo police. Yet he refused their offer of maximum security, scathingly arguing that it was a waste of public money. Officers tried to keep a discreet watch on him, but they could hardly disobey his orders. By today's standards, his personal security precautions were non-existent.

78-year-old Mountbatten publicly refused to be fazed by the prospect of becoming a key terrorist target. Asked a few months before his murder whether he was frightened of the IRA, he replied: 'What would they want with an old man like me?'

Tragically, the question would soon be answered.

One of the baffling things about his attitude was that he had learned the hard way the first rule of warfare. From his days as a 16-year-old midshipman in the World War I Battle of Jutland, the message had been rammed home again and again: 'Never underestimate your enemy.' No doubt Mountbatten knew the IRA's proven capabilities. He simply refused to let the threat of terrorism dominate his life.

It is also true that he was not a man who was easily cowed. For a period of World War II Mountbatten was commanding a Royal Navy destroyer flotilla on patrol in the North Atlantic. His flagship, 'HMS Kelly', was twice struck by mines and the Admiral in charge of operations decided that she could not be salvaged. Rather than risk the vessel falling into German hands, he signalled to Mountbatten: 'Abandon ship, I'm going to sink you.' The reply came back with lightning speed: 'Try it and I'll bloody well sink you.'

Mountbatten proved his point by nursing his ship safely home. Later 'HMS Kelly' would not be so lucky. She was sunk by German dive-bombers off Crete, and Mountbatten clung to wreckage for four hours in the water before he was rescued.

By now his career was on the fast-track. Churchill had spotted his cool head and impressive tactical know-how and appointed him Chief of Combined Operations with responsibility for planning the 1944 Allied invasion of Europe. Later he was made Supreme Allied Commander for south east Asia, accepting the Japanese surrender at Singapore.

In the post-war years, Mountbatten's reputation took a knock when, as Viceroy of India he engineered the British withdrawal by creating Pakistan for the Muslims and India for the Hindus. The arrangement was a disaster, reinforcing old hatreds and rivalries that persist to this day. It was said that Churchill, one of Mountbatten's closest friends, refused to speak to him for five years afterwards.

In the '60s, Mountbatten retired from his desk job at the Ministry of Defence. The deaths of his wife, Edwina, and Churchill affected him deeply but his spirit saw him through. After his retirement he devoted himself to his favourite past-times, meeting old friends, driving fast, walking, riding and fishing.

It was to fishing that he turned his attention on the morning of Monday, 27th August, 1979. At about 11.30 am he boarded the 'Shadow V' with members of his family and a local deck hand. The idea was to cruise up the coast of Donegal and check on a few lobster pots set earlier in the week. From there the party planned a slow trip back to harbour for a relaxed family dinner at the castle.

None of them could know that, early that morning, Provo member, Thomas McMahon, had slunk aboard to place a radio-controlled bomb below deck. Now McMahon was stationed on the cliffs above the bay watching the 'Shadow V' as she cut through the waves. A few minutes after noon he hit the detonation button.

Instantly a blinding flash heaved the vessel into the air and then scattered it into thousands of pieces. The roar was heard by fishing boats for miles around and within seconds skippers had their engines at full power as they headed for the mass of floating debris. Soon they were dragging survivors from the bloodstained water.

Mountbatten's grandson, Nicholas Brabourne, died instantly, as did the 15-year-old local hand, Paul Maxwell. Mountbatten himself lived for a few minutes longer, unconscious with pain, his legs almost torn away by the explosion. Lord Brabourne, his wife Patricia and another grandson, Timothy, all survived with terrible injuries. But Lord Brabourne's mother, the 82-year-old Dowager Lady Brabourne, died the following morning at Sligo General Hospital.

It was the first act in a day of carnage at the hands of the IRA. Later that afternoon, an Army lorry was blown up by a roadside bomb just inside the Ulster border. Survivors radioed for help but when a unit of the Queen's Own Highlanders, led by Lieutenant Colonel David Blair, arrived by helicopter they walked straight into a trap. A second bomb was detonated, killing Blair and eleven of his soldiers. More British servicemen died that day than in any other single attack since 1969.

So the IRA had their headlines and the Army Council milked the publicity for all it was worth. A statement read: 'The IRA claim responsibility for the execution of Lord Louis Mountbatten. This operation is one of the discriminate ways we can bring to the attention of the English people the continuing occupation of our country.' Later they warned the government that the joint attacks were designed to 'tear out their sentimental imperialist hearts.'

But it was not a total success for the Provos. Their bomber, McMahon, had been detained just three hours after he had detonated the bomb that killed Mountbatten. Irish police manning a roadblock were alerted by the nervous appearance of two men in a car. The driver was 24-year-old farmer, Francis McGill, and the passenger was Thomas McMahon.

Intelligence checks revealed that McMahon was a member of the IRA. Furthermore forensic tests showed up traces of nitroglycerine on his clothes, and sand matching that from the slipway at Mullaghmore was found on his boots. There were even minute flakes of green paint on his clothes, which matched the paint on the hull of 'Shadow V'. McMahon was later found guilty of the assassination and given a life sentence.

In the aftermath of Mountbatten's death, tributes to him poured in from world leaders. US President Jimmy Carter described himself as 'profoundly shocked and saddened' by the loss of a leader with 'monumental ability'. The Pope condemned the assassin whose actions, he said, were 'an insult to human dignity'. Predictably, Northern Irish Protestant gunmen turned on Northern Irish Catholics to fulfil a senseless revenge. And so the cycle of violence was given yet another spin.

Perhaps the greatest sadness for Mountbatten's family was not so much his death, but the manner of it. Here was a man who had survived the horrors of two World Wars, only to be killed as he tried to find peace in retirement. His last television interview, given to the BBC a few months earlier, contained the following remark: 'I do not mind death as long as it is a reasonably peaceful and satisfying sort of death.'

It was a humble enough wish. The IRA blew it away.

Anwar el-Sadat

The world watched with bated breath as Egyptian leader, Anwar el-Sadat, signed a momentous peace treaty with Egypt's long-time adversary, Israel.

When Sadat put his name to the document that signalled a possible end to bloodshed in the strife-torn Middle East, the West heaved a sigh of relief. Perhaps now the news pictures which flashed over the globe with alarming regularity, showing burnt-out tanks and dead bodies half-hidden in desert sand following yet another conflict between Arabs and Jews, could finally be dispatched to the archives of history.

The Muslim world, however, viewed matters differently. It was not infected with the same optimism and hope for the future. Rather, Islamic fundamentalists viewed Sadat as a dirty traitor who was cavorting with their bitterest foe. They vowed to make the President pay for this evil deed. When he scrawled his signature on the historic peace agreement, Sadat was signing his own death warrant.

Sadat was born on 25th December, 1918 in the delta of the Nile, where the world's longest river meets the Mediterranean Sea. When he was a child he developed a lifelong passion for the military. He had only one ambition, to join the Egyptian army, and this he achieved when he graduated from the Cairo Royal Military Academy in 1938. Like many of his countrymen, he was filled with loathing for the British forces in his land. In 1942, he was arrested by the British for espionage on behalf of the Nazis and subsequently jailed, although he soon slipped away from custody.

Anwar Sadat, the Egyptian peace-maker.

He liaised with Gamal Abdel Nasser, the dynamic patriot who organised the nationalist Free Officers organisation after World War II. Their hour for power finally came in 1952 when they toppled the monarchy. There was dancing in the streets when King Farouk, a corrupt playboy, abdicated and sailed out of Alexandria on a luxury yacht. Egypt remained in turmoil for two years until Nasser took the reins of power in 1954.

Under Nasser, Sadat became an important minister, serving two spells as Vice-President. He was a natural successor to the great leader, who died of a heart attack in September, 1970.

It was a hard act to follow. Nasser had commanded the respect and affection of his people. The welcome for Sadat was subdued among Egyptians who saw in him little of the vitality of his predecessor. Yet Sadat aimed to do much for his beloved country.

He risked everything when he struck against an unwary Israel in 1973 during an important Jewish festival. The Yom Kippur War was a success and renewed his standing at home. It was a time of great rejoicing in Egypt.

However, other policies which he pursued sparked disquiet. He veered away from the Soviet patronage which Nasser's socialist policies had attracted. Instead, he sought to establish closer links with the West. This was the key, he felt sure, to greater prosperity and hope for his country. America responded enthusiastically to his overtures, determined to seize the chance of a foothold in the Muslim world. Where better to start than Egypt, the most eminent of Arab states?

Sadat was also losing heart for the long-running battle between Arab and Jew in which thousands of lives were lost and precious little was gained. He was ripe for compromise and concession and astonished the world in 1977, when he accepted an invitation from Israeli Prime Minister Menachem Begin to speak before the Knesset, the Israeli parliament. It was a launch-pad for two years of shuttle diplomacy, which had American peace brokers travelling to and from the Middle East in search of an elusive settlement.

Their efforts were not in vain. In March, 1979 the Camp David peace accord was officially sealed. President Jimmy Carter, who watched the ceremonial signing on the lawn of the White House, declared: 'Peace has come. We have won, at last, the first step of peace, a first step on a long and difficult road.'

Even as the ink was drying on the peace accord, the voices of Arab demonstrators in a nearby park hung in the air. Their chant was: 'Sadat is a traitor.' The same message was echoing around the other Arab countries of the Middle East.

It was only two months since the Shah of Iran had been ousted by fanatical supporters of the Ayatollah Khomeini, and Muslims were revelling in a resurgence of pride and strength in Islam. The agreement with Begin dealt them a severe blow. There was talk of reprisals from many quarters. Other Arab governments considered taking retaliatory action against Egypt and Sadat, dismissing out of hand the gains made through the talks by Sadat. The arrival of Begin in Egypt a month later, the first Israeli prime minister to set foot in Cairo, added to the growing tension.

Sadat shared the 1978 Nobel Peace Prize with Menachem Begin for his ground-breaking peace initiative. Still, the array of Arab countries opposing him was unmoved.

It was clear that Sadat was a target for assassination by

any number of Islamic groups. His intelligence service issued worrying reports about the growing resentment towards him festering around Egypt. Ministers were bracing themselves for the coup they felt sure was brewing. Even Begin gave a warning to Sadat about the likelihood of a backlash.

Sadat realised, too, that the antics of his newest ally were causing alarm and anger in the Middle East. In the summer of 1981 Israel had launched a suprise air attack against a nuclear reactor in Iraq and claimed 150 lives in a ferocious strike on Beirut. Begin and his cronies were making talks of peace look pretty hollow.

At home, Sadat, on advice from his closest confidants, authorised a purge of fundamentalists in which one thousand six hundred people were rounded up. The die was cast. Yet the fatal attack on Sadat came when he was least expecting it. It was during the military march-past to commemorate victory in the Yom Kippur War that a handful of Muslims, led by army lieutenant Khaled Ahmed Shawkyal Islambouly, sought to avenge the Arab world.

Sadat usually relished the public holiday which was marked with a procession of military hardware and forces personnel. Close advisors have since claimed that the statesman was weary and deflated at the enmity aroused by his peace-keeping efforts before the parade of 6th October, 1981. Yet Sadat looked resplendent in his dark uniform decorated with gold braid and a green sash, flanked by eight bodyguards.

Before arriving at the celebration in Nasr City that day, he had already paid tribute at the graveside of Gamal Abdel Nasser and at the tomb of the unknown soldier. Travelling in a black, open-top Cadillac limousine, he arrived at the buzzing parade ground for the two hour celebration at 10 am. Guests included dignataries from home and abroad, military advisors, ambassadors and journalists. His wife, Jihan, was there, accompanied by several of their grandchildren.

The display was well underway when the assassins struck. Distracted, Sadat and many of his fellow guests had their eyes trained upwards on a formation flight of jets. If they had only looked forward, they would have spotted one of the Russian-built artillery trucks apparently stalling in front of the stand.

Without warning, the lieutenant leapt out and produced a hand grenade, which he unpinned and lobbed into the podium. It failed to explode, as did a second grenade. The third fell short of the stand and exploded on impact with the ground. Islambouly and his three cohorts then pointed their automatic rifles at Sadat and those alongside him. They advanced relentlessly, firing continuously.

Sadat had risen to greet his killers, at first believing them to be well-wishers. He was cut down by four bullets, blood spurting from his mouth.

Stunned by the suddenness of the attack, the guns of the presidential guards were silent for a few seconds before they burst into life. In the gun battle that followed eleven dignataries, including Sadat, were either killed outright or died of their wounds later in hospital. Among the victims were top-ranking government officials and a visiting prince from Oman. Thirty more were wounded.

Despite the chaos, a radio call went out for a helicopter, which arrived three minutes later to whisk the stricken President to Maadi military hospital. Doctors worked frantically to revive him, but to no avail. While the official time of death was given as 2.40 pm, it is certain that he gave up his hold on life before he arrived at the hospital.

One of the assassins unleashes a hail of bullets at President Anwar Sadat.

As for the killers, one was cut down within moments of opening fire. The survivors were arrested and stood trial with twenty others for murder and conspiracy. Lieutenant Islambouly and four conspirators were sentenced to death. The military men faced a firing squad while the civilians were hanged. A further seventeen received jail sentences and two were acquitted.

A Libyan backed group based in Tripoli soon claimed responsiblity for the murder. More likely candidates, however, were the extreme Muslim Brotherhood or fundamentalist Takfir Wal-Hajira (Repentance of the Holy Flight) which had been squeezed by the governments of Nasser and Sadat.

The aim was undoubtedly to wipe out Sadat and his regime, making way for a new and radical Muslim government. As such, the assassination was a failure.

The Western world was furious at the barbarity of the crime and was determined to see the historic peace accord remain in place. Britain's Prince Charles, French President Mitterand and three former US Presidents - Carter, Nixon and Ford - attended the funeral, held at the scene of the shooting.

Although there were celebrations at the killing in parts of the Muslim world, it didn't light the fuse of revolution in Egypt as the plotters had hoped. Instead, Sadat's deputy, Hosni Mubarak, a former commander in the Air Force and fighter pilot, was voted into office and vowed to stand by the Camp David agreement. Dreams of a brave new Muslim state had come to nought.

Benigno Aquino

The murder of Benigno Aquino was perhaps the most incompetent killing of modern times. For not since Julius Caesar has a political assassination backfired so quickly on its perpetrator.

Aquino was the main political opponent of the corrupt dictator of the Philippines, Ferdinand Marcos. And just as Caesar's death led to the ruin of his murderers, so Aquino's led to the demise and exile of Marcos and his wife, Imelda.

Benigno Aquino was born on 27th November, 1932, the son of well-to-do parents in Tarlac province. He began a career in journalism, but soon became involved in politics and, at the age of 22, he was elected Mayor of Concepcion. In 1959 he became vice-governor of Tarlac, taking over as governor two years later. In 1966 he was elected Secretary General of the Liberal party and the following year he became a senator.

The youngest ever mayor had become the youngest ever governor and the youngest ever senator. It seemed inevitable that, by the time he was 40, he would be the country's youngest president, because by then Ferdinand Marcos would have served the two terms allowed in the constitution and would have to step down. Aquino seemed to be the obvious successor.

Marcos and his wife, however, were not about to surrender the luxurious trappings of power quite so easily. On 23rd September, 1972 Marcos declared martial law and assumed a position that was his for as long as he wanted it: supreme commander of the country.

He immediately began a purge of his political opponents. First among these was Benigno Aquino, who was

Benigno Aquino died by official treachery as soon as he set foot in the Philippines, en route to a long-awaited reunion with his many loyal supporters.

accused of trumped-up charges of murder, rape, illegal possession of firearms and subversion. He was sentenced to death.

Strangely, Marcos did not execute Aquino immediately. Instead he had him kept in solitary confinement, where he maintained a correspondence with him for seven and a half years. Marcos kept trying to persuade Aquino to pledge that he would not oppose the Marcos regime, but over and over again, Aquino vowed that he would fight the tyrant.

Then Aquino developed heart trouble. United States President Jimmy Carter stepped in and asked Marcos to allow his enemy to have surgery in the United States. It was the perfect answer for Marcos. Aquino in exile would soon be forgotten. So the former senator moved to Boston with his wife Corazon. For three years he was an academic at Harvard, while conditions in the Philippines worsened

Meanwhile, the Carter administration, dedicated to human rights, gave way to that of Ronald Reagan, whose principal aim was the containment of communism. Marcos was seen by Washington as a key element in that policy. He was feted as a hero and a defender of democracy, even as his personal fortune swelled at the expense of his people, who were daily deprived of more liberties.

Martial law was finally lifted in 1981, when elections were held. Marcos was re-elected (despite the constitutional ban on a president serving more than two terms) amidst grave suspicion of ballot-rigging.

Aquino was becoming increasingly agitated in Boston, especially as Washington and Manila seemed to be getting closer and closer. By the time of the next parliamentary elections in 1983, it had become clear to him that, if the opponents of Marcos were to make any headway at all, he had to be there to lead them. He laid his plans and made his intentions clear. Then Imelda Marcos travelled to New York, where she met Aquino and gave him the clearest warning not to return.

'Ninoy,' she said, 'there are people loyal to us who cannot be controlled.'

Benigno Aquino ignored the chilling threat. He announced that he would return to Manila on a Japan Air Lines flight in August. Marcos warned that he would revoke the airline's landing rights if they took him, so JAL returned Aquino's fare and cancelled his flight with them.

Aquino finally ended his exile, flying a roundabout route home via China. But his final return was the worst kept secret in the country, because when he took off from Taiwan on the last leg of the journey, his supporters started moving in on Manila airport. The authorities also knew he was on the way. They sealed off the airport, keeping the twenty thousand strong crowd out of sight of the runway. The military took over all security, and as China Airlines Flight 811 made its final approach, it was met by a phalanx of soldiers and a ring of steel.

Aboard the plane, Aquino was surrounded by an entourage of aides, press and television crews. Nevertheless, as the plane touched down, he thought it advisable to put on a bullet-proof vest. 'My chances of surviving this trip are 10 per cent,' he had told a reporter on the flight. The bullet-proof vest was his attempt to improve them.

Three soldiers boarded the plane through the door at the front. They escorted Aquino to the rear, where a set of steel steps had been positioned. Aquino was smiling placidly as he accompanied his guards. The soldiers were grim-faced as they shoved the journalists back on the plane and smashed a television camera that was recording the scene.

The door was slammed shut as Aquino was taken out. Reporters who rushed to try to open it were beaten back by the guards. They scrambled to the plane's windows.

First they heard a shot. Then a fusillade. Those able to reach the windows saw Benigno Aquino lying face down on the tarmac with blood spurting from a bullet hole in the back of his head. Nearby lay another body dressed in the blue overalls of an airport worker. Three troopers were firing round after round into this corpse. The soldiers who had taken Aquino off the plane were nowhere to be seen.

The government immediately put out a statement that a lone gunman had been responsible for Aquino's death, and that the killer had been shot by security forces. It was days before the supposed assassin was identified as Rolando Galman, a Manila police sergeant. Aquino was dead, but Marcos had overreached himself ....

As thirty thousand mourners filed past Aquino's glass-topped coffin, and more than a million supporters followed his funeral cortege, chanting 'Democracy, freedom, revolution', it was obvious to the world that the assassination story was a cover-up. How could one man acting alone have pierced such an elaborate security blanket? How could he have known his target was leaving the plane by the rear rather than by the passenger tube at the front?

At last even the Reagan administration was forced to accept the likelihood of Marcos' complicity, and they started to put pressure on him. Marcos announced an inquiry, which fourteen months later revealed that Galman had been set up, that Aquino had been shot from behind by security guards and that the plans were laid by military commander General Fabian, Marcos' cousin.

A total of twenty-six people were prosecuted in a blatantly rigged trial. Not surprisingly, all were found not guilty.

In 1986, Marcos announced an early general election. Aquino's wife, Corazon (Cory) Aquino, led the opposition to Marcos. She announced that she would depose the president and put him on trial for the murder of her husband.

By the time the election had taken place, Marcos had just one friend left in the corridors of world power: Ronald Reagan. And Reagan continued to support the tyrant, even after it had become blatantly obvious to the rest of the world that Marcos had again rigged the ballots and stolen the election. But even Reagan had to take action after the emergence of a genuine surge of support for Cory Aquino, the defection of units of the Philippines military and further evidence linking Marcos to the death of Benigno Aquino.

On 25th February, 1986, faced with the loss of American support abroad and a revolution at home, Marcos fled in disgrace to Hawaii with Imelda and his cousin, General Ver. He was to live out the rest of his life in luxury, but would die in exile.

Meanwhile, Cory Aquino became president and the country's Supreme Court overturned the acquittals of those tried following the death of her husband. Sixteen of them began life sentences soon afterwards.

Cory Aquino's presidency had some triumphs, but finally she was overcome by political and economic problems. When her popularity waned and she was removed from office, however, it was through the democratic process. Official acts of terrorism and political assassinations had become largely a thing of the past in the Philippines.

One man's death had made all this possible.

Indira and Rajiv Gandhi

It seemed as if Indira Gandhi and her son, Rajiv, had the perfect credentials for the demanding task of ruling India. They were from a distinguished line of politicians which had run like a golden thread through the history of the young state.

Indira's father was Jawaharial Nehru, the first Prime Minister of India after it won independence in 1947, and highly respected both at home and abroad. Her aunt was Vijaya Lakshmi Pandit, another leading light in the campaign to free her country from colonial rule. She went on to be ambassador to the Soviet Union, ambassador to the USA, president of the UN General Assembly and high commissioner to the UK. Indira's grandfather was Motilal Nehru, ex-president of the Indian National Congress, the party which had sought freedom from British rule.

Strife had dogged the fledgling nation, however, from the moment it raised its flag aloft. Despite their noble and impressive heritage, Indira and Rajiv presided over a country torn in dozens of different directions. Both made heavy-handed judgements about some of their most volatile minorities. And mother and son paid for those decisions with their lives.

Indira Gandhi was born in 1917 and benefited from a fine education in England and Switzerland. She married Feroz Gandhi (no relation to the fêted Mahatma Gandhi) in 1942. There is evidence that the marriage quickly went off the rails, due to Indira's whole-hearted dedication to the world of politics, steered as she was by her accomplished father.

After Nehru died, Indira became a cabinet minister

Indira Gandhi, the matriarch of Mother India, was gunned down by two of her guards.

under prime minister Lal Bahadur Shastri and emerged as leader of both Congress Party and country in 1966. Perhaps there was a belief among the elders of the party that she would be no more than an acceptable figurehead. In fact, she threw off the shadow of her father and soon became the manipulator rather than being manipulated.

In 1971 she won a sweeping general election victory with the potent slogan of 'garivo hatao' (abolish poverty). Her international standing was also high, thanks to her achievements in brokering peace between Pakistan and East Pakistan and easing the creation of Bangladesh.

However, a backlash was brewing which would sweep her from this pedestal. In 1975 an Indian court found that the 1971 election had been rigged. Instead of gracefully stepping down, Indira clung to power with a draconian clampdown. Thousands of her opponents were jailed after a state of emergency was declared and she tolerated not the smallest whiff of dissent. Her 'big stick' approach alienated hordes of her people. When it came to the general election of 1977, Indira, to her horror, was routed by Morarji Desai, leader of the Janata Party.

For three years the Janata party tried and failed to run India. At the next election, Indira was re-elected, welcomed with open arms by the people. The joyous time was blighted when her youngest son Sanjay, whom she was grooming to inherit her position, died in an air crash. She looked to her eldest son, airline pilot Rajiv, to fill his shoes.

As leader, however, her dilemmas remained the same. The religious factions under her control still pulled away from Mother India. She remained committed to keeping India as one country.

After her re-election, the Sikhs, who formed the majority in the Punjab region, mounted increasing pressure for an independent state of Khalistan. The extremists decided to make their case by occupying the Golden Temple of Amritsar, a revered Sikh shrine as well as an important Hindu site.

Indira made a bold but possibly foolhardy decision in ordering her troops to confront the rebels. Operation Blue Star in June, 1984 achieved its aim, which was to oust the Sikhs. But the cost was dangerously high. The Sikhs put up a ferocious fight. At the end seven hundred of them lay dead in addition to ninety soldiers. As wave after wave of soldiers was repelled, the army sent in commandos and tanks, causing extensive damage to this, the most holy of Sikh places. Sant Jarnail Singh Bhindranwale, the leader of the zealots, was among the dead.

Nationwide, there was outrage with a burst of reprisals by angry Sikhs. Indira Gandhi's life was clearly under threat. Even so, she maintained a number of Sikhs in her bodyguard, apparently certain of their loyalty.

Five months after the bloodshed, her faith in those guards proved tragically misplaced. As Indira walked from her home to her office on 31st October, 1984, clad in a yellow sari and anticipating an interview with actor Peter Ustinov, she smiled at the two Sikh guards she knew and liked. But both Beant Singh and Satwant Singh had been willingly recruited as assassins following the desecration of the Golden Temple.

Beant Singh, a long time guard of the prime minister, blasted her with three bullets from his revolver. His accomplice Satwant Singh then turned on her with a sten gun, riddling her body with bullets.

Indira collapsed in a bloodied heap. Her 66-year-old body had suffered ten bullet wounds. She was rushed to hospital, held in the arms of her daughter-in-law, Sonia,

Rajiv Gandhi was reluctantly sworn into office within hours of his mother's death.

but could not be saved.

Retribution had already been meted out against assassin Beant Singh. As police surrounded him, he yelled 'I have done what I wanted to do. Now do as you please.' They shot him dead.

Satwant was injured, but survived and stood trial, to be hung later for his part in the killing. The investigation into the conspiracy eventually implicated top government aides and even hinted at international intrigue. Later, a minister suggested that neighbouring Pakistan had aided the embittered Sikhs in a bid to destablise rival India.

Ironically, the violent death of Indira Gandhi was no more than she herself had expected. The day before her death she told a meeting 'If I die today, every drop of my blood will invigorate the nation.'

The reluctant Rajiv was sworn into office within hours. His first days as premier were a baptism of fire. Hindus were furious at the murder of Indira and wreaked a terrible revenge against the Sikh population. Despite his pleas for calm, indiscriminate rioting and killing continued as 40-year-old Rajiv wrestled with the mantle of power.

Barely a month later, a gas leak at Bhopal claimed the lives of two thousand people and injured scores more. Nevertheless, Rajiv was returned to power by the voters in an election held at the end of 1984. He was prime minister for five years before losing power and having to fight an election to regain office in 1991. Gone was the reserved manner which used to be his hallmark. In its place was a relaxed, affable manner, a new-found charm which he was wielding to beguile doubters and 'don't knows'.

India was still a hotch-potch of grievances. The Tamils, a group originally from the island of Sri Lanka, who wanted independence from India, feared repression from Rajiv

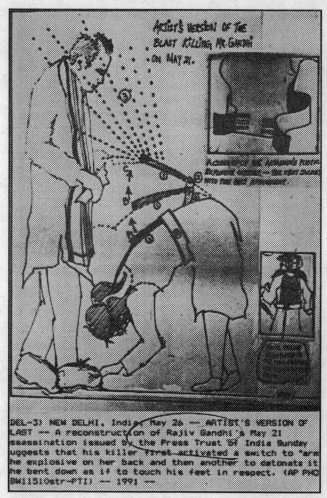

Death of a president: Rajiv Gandhi's assassin activated the explosives she carried on her back - then bent down as if to touch his feet in respect.

if he were re-elected. Extremists vowed to end the threat once and for all. To do so, they employed a loyal woman who was willing to be turned into a human bomb. Known only as Dhanu, she was wired up with belts containing plastic explosives and detonators for a kamikaze mission.

The Tamils knew only too well that Rajiv was accessible as never before, thanks to his new image. On 21st May, 1991 Dhanu was among thousands who assembled to hear Rajiv speak at Sriperumbudur, in the heartland of his party's stronghold.

Father of two Rajiv was being decorated with garlands and expected nothing else from the woman who bowed down before him in reverence. In fact, she was pushing a button on her belt which would not only kill her target and herself but also seventeen others around them. It was a scene of grim devastation. People who seconds before had been revelling in a good-natured rally were blown to pieces.

Once again there was a magnificently coloured and heady funeral procession followed by a cremation on a pyre. India was again consumed with anger and violence.

The Tamil leaders responsible for the outrage had, for the most part, fled the country or gone to ground. Police doggedly pursued them but they were unwilling prisoners. In total, twenty-two killed themselves to avoid justice.

Rajiv's Italian born wife, Sonia, who had long feared an assassination attempt on her husband, was reverently offered a key role in government. She turned it down. So the assassin's bomb which claimed so many lives finally ended a political dynasty spanning four generations.

The dreams harboured by Indira Gandhi for her family's future at the helm of India were blown to bits.